T M

The Secular Journal of

THOMAS MERTON

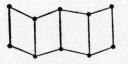

Farrar, Straus & Giroux

NEW YORK

Preface

¶ The fact that these pages are being published after a
lapse of twenty years may require a few words of ex-
planation. These are a few selections taken from a
diary that I kept when I was a layman, a graduate
student at Columbia, teaching in University Exten-
sion there, and later when I was an Instructor at St.
Bonaventure University. This was written, like most
diaries, informally, colloquially, and in haste. The
whole diary filled two or three large manuscript
volumes. Only one of these still exists, the others were
thrown away or destroyed after I had typed out a
few excerpts which are given here, along with parts
of the surviving volume.

The typed manuscript which furnishes the material
for the present book was given by me to Catherine de
Hueck Doherty, the foundress of Friendship House,
Harlem, when I decided to enter the monastery of

Gethsemani. Neither one of us had much hope that
the book would find a publisher, but in case it did I
told Catherine that all the rights belonged to her,
and that if the book ever turned out to be worth anything, she could use it to help her in her work in
Catholic Action.

Years went by, and I managed to get some other
books published. I had completely forgotten about
this Journal until one day in 1955 a letter from
Catherine reminded me of it. She asked me if I had
changed my mind about letting her sell it to a publisher. Obviously I had not: the manuscript was hers
to do with as she pleased, and if someone wanted to
publish it, then I was delighted to let her take this
opportunity to profit by it. However, we have not
rushed into print thoughtlessly. The manuscript re-
quired some editing. The problem was to avoid destroying or notably altering the artless spontaneity of
the original, to keep its somewhat naïve essence, and
yet to correct its more intolerable defects. Perhaps
some readers may feel that the book is still intolerable. If so, we heartily regret the fact. In any case,
the careless style, the callow opinions and all the
other defects are those of a writer much younger and
even more unwise than I am at present.

Certainly the views and aspirations expressed, at

times, with such dogmatic severity, have come to be softened and tempered with the passage of time and with a more intimate contact with the spiritual problems of other people. I hope I may be forgiven for having allowed some of my youthful sarcasms to survive in these pages. To have cut them all out completely would have been a falsification of the whole book. An indulgent reader will still perhaps be inclined to consider them funny and *à propos*. I hope so. In any case, here they are! It should be quite clear that all this was written before I entered the monastery, and in no way claims to represent the outlook of the Cistercian Order of the Strict Observance to which I belong. This is not the work of a monk or of a priest, but of a young layman recently converted to the Catholic faith and still struggling to find out whether or not he was supposed to dedicate his life to writing or to some higher and more special vocation. It is quite obviously not what one normally calls "spiritual reading."

Since this work, and any royalties it may earn, belong to Catherine de Hueck Doherty's "Madonna House," it might be well to introduce the reader to both the Foundress and her foundation. Baroness Catherine de Hueck fled from Russia when the

Reds took over in 1917. She was still only a child. When I first met her her friends still called her "the Baroness" or more familiarly "B." Readers of *The Seven Storey Mountain* will remember her under this name. The title of nobility has since vanished into oblivion, and rightly. Never on the face of this earth was there ever anyone *less* of an effete aristocrat than Catherine. Her boundless, earthy solidity and her deep faith are those of a peasant. I always remember her as one of the most energetic and generous people I have ever met—and one of the most simple. Everything she says and does is quite direct, and she never pulls any of her punches. She goes straight to the heart of the issue. The revolution had made her poor. Far from resenting the fact, she embraced it with prodigious good humor and fervent thanksgiving as a marvelous grace from God. She resolved to make poverty her vocation with a vigor and directness that are thoroughly Franciscan.

She is not the kind of person that gets overexcited at the thought of communism. The Reds do not upset her, and never will. She has lived for forty years as a proletarian and she can size up communism with the shrewd common sense of the worker of the western world who has learned that not everything that comes out of Russia is necessarily good or necessarily evil. She knows that if there was a revolution in Russia, there were reasons for one: she has not ceased to believe in cause and effect, just because the revolution happened to enter, quite brutally, into her own personal life. She knows from experience why communism to some extent appeals to certain elements in the western working class, and to some extent repels them. Above all, because she is a Christian, she is thoroughly aware of the futility and inner contradictions of a dialectic that is purely materialistic. The Reds do not worry her, because she knows that they will end up in another one of those ashcans, further down the street of history.

But at the same time, she is one who feels that Christianity cannot and must not be a mere matter of fine words and pretty speeches at Communion breakfasts. She knows that it is the business of Christians to point out the fallacy of communism not merely by their words, but by their lives: and this is not merely a matter of one's personal virtues, but of social conscience. Our duty as Christians does not end with the salvation of our own souls. We are debtors not only to God but to our neighbor, and Jesus Himself made it very clear that our neighbor is not just the one who lives in the apartment next door. The Parable of the Good Samaritan teaches us

that everyone who suffers, everyone who is unjustly
treated, who is oppressed, cheated, forgotten, or neglected, is our neighbor. And we have to love him as
we love ourselves. It is no good to pass by on the
other side of the road with our eyes devoutly cast
down, with our lips murmuring pious prayers—and
with plenty of money jingling in our pockets. More
than that, Catherine is one who realizes more clearly
than almost anyone I know, that her neighbor is not
only her neighbor but he is also Christ. To love,
serve and help our brother, is to love, serve and help
Christ. She is one to whom the doctrine of the Mystical Body is something more than a stimulating theory.

This was one of the things she learned when she
was working in a laundry and sharing her meager
lunch with a fellow worker, as they sat together on
the steps of a dingy brownstone house, in a New York
slum district in the twenties. This was what moved
her to start Friendship House, in Toronto, in 1930.
This, too, was what brought her to Harlem in 1938,
with nothing but a couple of dollars and a typewriter.
She moved into a tenement on 135th Street, and
Friendship House had entered the United States!

I met Catherine in 1941. The results of the meet-
ing are recorded in these pages. She was then working almost entirely on interracial justice, in Harlem,

and preparing to branch out to Chicago's South Side.
But Friendship House was, to her, something more.
It was the beginning of Madonna House—a center of
the lay apostolate in all fields: not only that of interracial justice, not only in rural areas, not only in the
missions—but everywhere. The idea had not yet fully
matured in those days. It has now.

Madonna House was founded in 1947 in the pine
forests of the Ottawa valley. Madonna House, at
Combermere, Ontario, is the center and cradle of the
new institute. It consists of a group of farms and cabins
which serve as the center of a fervent rural apostolate
and as a place of training for candidates wishing to
become members. At Combermere you will find just
about everything imaginable. It is an exciting place,
full of promise, seething with new and still barely
developed potentialities: social service, nursing and
ambulance service for the rural area, a library service
which reaches all parts of Canada by mail, a clothing
center, adult education courses, recreation facilities,
a Catholic Action summer school, a rest home for
priests. . . . Perhaps the simplest thing to do would
be to let Madonna House describe its own objectives.
These words are from a leaflet written by Catherine:

> *The goal of the Institute, as far as its works are con-
> cerned, is the broad Social Apostolate of the Church. It*

*stands ready to answer the call of the Ordinary of any dio-
cese in the world and to work in any phase of the Lay
Apostolate. Among these are included the rural apostolate, missionary work, work among working classes, work
with youth, information and catechetical centers, etc. It is
ready to undertake most of the works dealing with "the
masses"—especially in hard-to-get-at places, to which few
people wish to go.**

That gives you some idea of what Madonna House
stands for, what it is trying to do, what it will one
day be! Already it has branches in Alberta, in the
Indian missions of the Yukon territory, in the diocese
of Portland, Oregon, and in an Arizona town where
a mixed population of Mexicans, Navajos, Hopis
and Negroes are treated more or less as pariahs by
the rest of the world.†

When I was writing some of the final pages of this
diary in 1941, I was on the point of joining Catherine
de Hueck at Friendship House. She had asked me to
come, and the decision had been provisionally taken
—until it became clear that my vocation lay else-

---

* Anyone interested in this and other leaflets about the Institute may
obtain them by writing to Madonna House, Combermere, Ontario,
Canada.

†The situation regarding the mission houses has changed (1977). In
addition to the ones mentioned by Merton, there are also houses in
the West Indies, Cleveland, Ohio, Ottawa, and in Regina and Gravel-
bourg, Saskatchewan.

where: in a Cistercian monastery. Nevertheless, I
owe much to Catherine, and I am glad that this book
can help Madonna House in some way. The sale of
this volume may mean many things to the workers at
Combermere: a new car in which nurses can reach
outlying farms, or perhaps a new building, to house
the novices of the Institute. It may mean the difference between life and death to someone in Canada,
in the Yukon, in Arizona. It may mean the difference
between bitterness and peace, to many souls who
will be helped by Catherine and her workers. It may
mean the salvation of many souls who cannot be
reached until their bodily needs are first taken care of.

With all these things in mind, my Superiors have
agreed to allow the publication of this book, their
only conditions being that it should be examined
and approved by the censors of the Order, and that
the reader be told, quite clearly, that it was written
twenty years ago, before my entrance into the Abbey
of Gethsemani.

PART 1

Perry Street, New York

[WINTER: 1939–1940]

¶ When William Blake told somebody his poems
were dictated to him by the angels, he did not mean
that all other poetry was merely written by men, and
was therefore inferior to his own. On the contrary,
he meant that all good poetry was poetry dictated
by the angels, and that he himself could not claim
any particular praise for the poems he had written
because they were not exclusively his own.

But now that we believe as an article of faith that
man is the highest of all creatures, and is at the top
of the ladder of evolution, we have to be very care-
ful and guard our position against anything above
that—angels, or God. Under such circumstances, to
presume that poetry could be dictated to man by
someone above him is a terrific affront. And since
angels are mythical symbols, as we believe, in our
doghouse of ideas, Blake seems to be saying, in a
symbolic way, that he is the best of poets.

5

To say that your poems are dictated by the angels, if you don't believe in angels, is proud (it is just saying you yourself are pretty good!): but if you do believe in angels the statement is perfectly humble. And Blake believed in angels.

But what Blake was asserting was that he was at least a poet, while other writers (Klopstock, for example), who did not listen to the angels but wrote their own stuff, were not even poets. And to be a poet, especially as good a poet as Blake was, and not recognize it would be a totally false humility. If a man is a poet and doesn't recognize it, then he is either lying or else he is not lying. If he is lying he is a liar, which no poet should ever be, and if he is not lying then it is true, and he isn't a poet, and that's all right too. There is enough humility in poets from the moment they know that they are poets: because if they are, then they have to write in fear and trembling (as Blake told Samuel Palmer).

¶ To anybody but a Jansenist, Dante's *Paradiso* has to be the best of the three books of THE DIVINE COMEDY. The opening is more splendid than anything he has written before it. He starts by praying to achieve a much higher kind of writing than in the *Hell* and *Purgatory,* to fit this much higher subject: and he succeeds.

Everything is now made plain at once, everything has now become easy. Movements through space are swift and arrow-like, and the "keel" of the verse cuts the sea in a swift, straight furrow. There are no more elaborately hard images, no more distortions. Of course, the content is much more difficult than in the other books, but its treatment is correspondingly simpler.

Perhaps it is easier to write well of a difficult progress, like the arduous climbing through Purgatory than of the swift, breath-taking movement

through the nine spheres of heaven, a movement
nevertheless at the same time dignified as it is swift.

It is easier to communicate a clear idea of the
obscurity of hell than a clear idea of the clarity and
brilliance of heaven.

But the subject of the *Paradiso* is so much better
a subject than that of the other two books, that if the
writing only comes up to the material, this third
book must necessarily be the best of the three. (Those,
including the Victorian commentators who preferred
the *Inferno* before all three and the *Purgatory* next,
generally were bored by the very subject matter of
heaven: a rueful sort of state to die in!)

Close to the beginning of the *Paradiso* is a very
interesting image. It is used to describe how Dante
becomes acclimatised to the terrific intellectual brilliance of heaven, through the mediation of Beatrice.
He looks in her eyes at the reflection of what she sees,
until his eyes, from learning to stand the brilliance
of hers, are lost in the love of heaven's brilliance itself. And then he brings in a pagan analogy, in this
very vital spot, so effective that it knocks you out of
your chair:

Nel suo aspetto tal dentro mi fei
  Qual si fe' Glauco nel gustar dell' erba
Che il fe' consorto in mer degli altri dei.

8

He changes like Glaucus, who having eaten some strange, rare sea-grass became immortal and like the gods of the sea. What is the effect of this pagan image at this crucial transition point where Dante is entering the bliss of heaven? Glaucus is a character who, from being a half-known, obscure fisherman, was metamorphosed into the obscurest kind of god, something very remote, in the deep sea. He has vanished from the earth to live in an element obscure and weird and dumb where everything is like a strange dream. He leaves behind him on earth only a half-imaginable memory. He has gone to a remote and serious and almost abstract kind of bliss. What are his eternal sports, in the sea? Things strange to us, we cannot understand them. He got there by mistake, by eating grass.

All this feeling of remoteness, together with a sense of longing for some remote kind of peace, is carried by the Wordsworth lines where he wants to

Have sight of Proteus rising from the sea
Or hear old Triton blow his wreathed horn.

"Have sight of"—that is, Proteus is rarely seen. You have to catch a lucky glimpse of him, out in the sea, like a dolphin.

All the old pagan sea deities, the minor ones, are

9

creatures that appear distantly in the midst of their fantastic joys in the sea: and anything that is distant and at the same time beautiful, in poetry, arouses our intense interest and even desire. By bringing in Proteus and Triton, Wordsworth successfully evokes all kinds of unsatisfied longings for peace. And Dante very happily uses this same kind of trick, here.

In this case, the line carries with it an oblique statement of all the intense longing for heaven which is now going to be satisfied in Dante. The comparison is neither irreverent nor blasphemous, because it is the most effective way of making that statement. If he had said, "O how I had longed to be in heaven, and now . . ." he would have made a much less interesting statement. But now he says he felt himself transformed like Glaucus!

¶ Some beavers, in Connecticut, have built a dam and are flooding a lot of roads. The highway department of the county where this disaster is taking place has brought the matter to court, asking for the power to remove these audacious beavers.

The Attorney General, in Hartford, hands down a decision making this possible, by saying that rights of rational animals are inferior to those of the state, and therefore the rights of beavers are just that much more inferior to the rights of the state. Therefore, the beavers have to get out.

On the other hand, the beavers also have rights, and therefore "these little animals should be compensated." They will be removed to another home, where they will be "able to perform and exercise their natural skill and ability." I am sure there is some legal subtlety that makes this phrasing of the highest importance: "perform and exercise."

Wouldn't it be too bad if he forgot one of the words, and somebody took advantage of the decision and, while permitting the beavers to perform their natural skill, maliciously made it impossible for them to exercise it. Or what if someone brutally refused them the right to exercise their ability, but without, at the same time, interfering with their skill!

This hierarchy, *beavers: rational animals: state,* is just abstract enough to make me feel disturbed by the whole story. I wish they had kicked out the beavers without such a lot of talk: because obviously no court is going to bother with the rights of beavers anyway, not really. How can a court make itself responsible for dealing out justice to beavers?

If it pretends to, it makes you wonder how serious they are in dealing out justice to men.

I have no doubt the beavers have certain natural "rights," but I have every doubt whether those rights can be protected by a human court of law as if they were the rights of human beings. And what are the rights of these beavers? Life, liberty and the pursuit of happiness? The court said they had a right to perform and exercise their natural skill and ability.

I suppose the same can be said of rabbits. But also I suppose the rights of rabbits are not eternally fixed: they vary according to whether or not the hunting season is on. When it is closed, they have a right to life and the performance, etc. of their skills (which are all very elementary, to be sure), and when the season is open they lose all their rights.

I don't suppose even a State supreme court could go so far as to puzzle over the rights of rabbits in relation to foxes. Let us take it for granted that irrational animals have rights before men who are capable of making judgments, but not before other animals.

Even if beavers have rights (which I don't doubt), it doesn't do you any good to talk about them, or to guarantee them, or anything of the sort. On the contrary, to make a big argument over the rights of beavers is a suspicious enough joke to cast doubt on the validity of the rights of men.

There is one very simple way of dealing with beavers: not according to rights, but according to love. If you love God you will respect His creatures, and respect all life because it comes from Him, and you won't waste so much time talking about the rights of irrational beings.

But admittedly a law court is not designed to take care of questions insofar as they can be decided by love: that is the difference between a court and a confessional. So let it pass.

¶ One of the best things at the World's Fair Art Ex-
hibit is Fra Angelico's "Temptation of St. Anthony"
(also the Hieronymus Bosch of the same subject,
which is completely different). The saint is in the middle of a landscape of dry gullies, with trees and a city
in the background, and is being tempted by—a leaf
blowing on the dry ground. Anyway, he is startled,
and the drapery of his cloak and cassock, his arms, are
all in movement. It is a very perfect and dignified
movement like something in a solemn and ritualistic
dance, his face is calm and a little sad, the way old
Greek statues were. And behind him is a bright red
church on a hill, and some towers against a perfectly
luminous sky as clear as glass. There is the enamelled,
dark foliage of a line of trees, stunted by foreshorten-
ing.

Just as a prayer leads to stillness and timelessness in
contemplation, so the action of this picture leads to

contemplation on an esthetic level. Therefore looking at a picture demands penetration, understanding,
meditation. If people looked at good pictures more,
they would learn more about meditation, and if they
meditated more they would learn more about looking
at pictures.

In time, we follow out an action from its beginning
to its end, from the moment it is insensibly born out
of some other action until it is lost insensibly in yet
another action, meaning something else again. Our
experience is all made up of movements merging into
one another, never perfect, never meaning as much as
we want them to, never as satisfactory as we desire
them to be. But in eternity there is no transition between perfect significance and perfect significance.
Good pictures imitate eternity. They are stopped dead
at their most meaningful point: but that is the trouble, they are stopped *dead*.

The kind of movement in this picture, again, is the
most perfect movement, because it does not spend itself and vanish, but generates itself over and over by
its own stillness and significance. The best thing a man
can do on earth is to create things with this perfect
kind of action, pictures, or ideas, or prayers, or cathe-
drals, or monasteries or even perfect factories, why
not? Except that so far most factories, even when they

are mechanically perfect, are so inhuman (because of the stupefying and exhausting and unrewarded work imposed on the workmen) that we cannot easily visualise perfect factories in the same category as perfect pictures. If the people who run factories and the people who work in them ever get to be good and smart in the same way Angelico was, we will see some perfect factories also.

By realizing what constitutes the action in a good picture, we can get some sort of analogical grasp of what the joys of the blessed are in heaven. Not, of course, in the sense that the blessed are all sitting around open mouthed filling their eyes with actual colors and lights, because a person who only gathers up the sense impressions off the surface of a picture is enjoying it merely in the most elementary and unsatisfactory way. But the intellectual grasp of some kind of perfection, which gives us pleasure when we look at a picture with our minds working, as well as our senses, gives us some basis for talking analogically about the joys of heaven.

The Breughel wedding-dance in the same exhibition is also a very perfect picture. It is gay, not because of its subject matter but principally because of its form. The drunken gaiety of the people twists their faces up with pain rather than joy, and their dancing

is heavy and crude and unhappy, in itself. They are
not happy, they are merely drunk. But the picture is
very happy.

The basis of the composition is a pyramidal arrangement of people formed by the central dance and the
perspective of barns and sheds and so on, and at the
apex of this pyramid come two couples drawn as flat
as Thurber pictures. A line of spectators closes off the
right-hand side of the dance, curving down to the
pipers in the lower right-hand corner, and behind the
line is a crowd that seems, at first, to be just a crowd,
but which suddenly becomes very animated with red
kerchiefs and white aprons arranged in what would
make an interesting abstraction all by itself. The first
pyramid of dancers is carried on right into the back of
the canvas by trees, people, etc., and suddenly you no-
tice, at the apex of this pyramid, like the keystone of
the whole picture, one, rigid, solitary, little man in
grey with his back to the whole business, simply looking away at nothing, off at the back and top of the
picture. He is paying no attention to anything, doing
nothing, just standing, ignoring everything of the
subject matter, and yet being an essential element in
the construction of the whole picture; this is a sort of
humorous trick you sometimes find in Picasso, something that is a sort of a joke, in terms of subject matter,

17

yet is extremely important from the point of view of form.

In finding this man, I had found a key to a whole area of the picture that had gone completely unnoticed by me until then. My eye travelled back and discovered a whole barn full of people that I hadn't seen at all. And then, also, I began to find out just how much Breughel had done with his pattern of white aprons and caps and kerchiefs among the browns and reds of the figures. It made the picture very modern looking, not that there is any modern painter of the kind of subject matter that is capable of coming anywhere near this kind of success, but the arrangement of whites, browns, and reds, and the shapes of the areas of these colors are easily seen under the aspect of a modern abstraction.

This was, also, a popular picture. To begin with it was big and lively, and couldn't be missed. Everybody that went hurrying by feverishly reading the titles off the plaques on the frames at least paused here for a second and made some kind of remark or grunt or something. Maybe they only thought they liked it for the subject matter: but who cares, so long as they liked it? Probably the ones who had read two pages of art criticism somewhere also believed they liked this because it is "earthy" and "real," and yet that isn't the

reason at all why the picture is so gay. Modern painters
who know nothing but earthiness, never manage to be
anything but dull, yet they are four times as earthy as
Breughel ever was: so earthy that they are all clogged
up with their painstakingly acquired dirt.

But what were the people saying about this picture?
Two girls, art students probably: "It looks like one of
the early French Impressionists."

One Killer-of-a-Fellow, with a mob of female ad-
mirers: "Excellent reporting: look at those knees."
(The knees were very knobby.)

One of two girls (giggling): "Look at them kissing,
there."

A man: "That one's drunk, I guess."

Another Killer: "You can tell it's a Dutch painting:
not a skinny one in the whole bunch."

A man (foreign accent): "Country dance!"

A woman: "Look at those white aprons."

A man: "Some paunch!"

A man: "Look at the pipers."

There were a lot of people who just read off the
name, "Broo-gul," and walked on unabashed. But at
least they must have thought it important. They came
across with the usual reaction of people who don't
know pictures are there to be enjoyed, but think they
are things that have to be learned by heart to impress

the bourgeoisie: so they tried to remember the name.

In the first rooms, where the Angelicos were, there was a boy of eighteen or so, passing slowly from picture to picture with an older man. At each picture, the boy said: "The hands are good." At the Angelico "Annunciation" he said, of the angel: "One hand is better than the other," but the older man contradicted him, saying: "No, both hands are good."

While I was looking at the "Temptation of St. Anthony," which is, intellectually speaking, immensely gay, because of the light and purity of the form, I heard an old lady with a fairly harsh voice saying behind me, "Look, nobody laughs in these pictures. They must have been mighty unhappy people in those days."

In the El Greco room, people were shocked beyond measure, violent and bitter, especially women. Their voices got shrill with fear and indignation, and one old woman cried out: "They're all dying of the TB."

Of course there were plenty of comments on the misery and unhappiness of the age the painter lived in. What would be the good of turning around and asking the old lady: "If the world was dying then, what do you suppose it is doing now, in this age of hypochondriacs and murderers and sterilisers? How about *our* pictures, are they dying of anything? Or can

they be said to die, when they can't even come to life
in order to do so?"

It was not the fault of the people themselves, not
the result, that is, of ill-will—yet the comments in the
El Greco room were often horrifying. It seemed that
the religious pictures sometimes shocked people into
talking not like people, but like the possessed.

¶ What is the "mild yoke" of Christ's service?

The love of God is blessedness and joy. We love God, on earth by imitating Him, and it gives us great joy to be like Christ as much as we can. Unhappiness comes to us when we realize how unlike Him we are, and when we see that we are not imitating Him, and not doing His will, but only our own. It is the yoke of His service, that is doing His will as perfectly as we can, that is mild; but *not* to do His will, and *not* to accept His mild yoke, that is what is hard, and what kills us with sorrow.

What is doing His will: just doing anything we like, and saying it is His will?

It is keeping the greatest of the commandments, which includes all the others: "Thou shalt love the Lord thy God with thy whole heart, and thy neighbor as thyself."

Loving one another: this is the mild yoke of Christ's

service. But the hard yoke we are yoked under is the yoke of our own pride and self-love, loving our own good and our neighbor's evil, and loving only the limited good which we enjoy at our neighbor's expense.

November 2, 1939

ALL SOULS

¶ There is a logic of language and a logic of mathematics. The former is supple and lifelike, it follows our experience. The latter is abstract and rigid, more ideal. The latter is perfectly necessary, perfectly reliable: the former is only sometimes reliable and hardly ever systematic. But the logic of mathematics achieves necessity at the expense of living truth, it is less real than the other, although more certain. It achieves certainty by a flight from the concrete into abstraction. Doubtless, to an idealist, this would seem to be a more perfect reality. I am not an idealist.

The logic of the poet—that is, the logic of language or the experience itself—develops the way a living organism grows: it spreads out towards what it loves, and is heliotropic, like a plant. A tree grows out into a free form, an organic form. It is never ideal, only free; never typical, always individual.

St. Augustine's philosophy follows the logic of ex-

24

perience and literary expression. His dialectic moves
and grows of its own life, and grows toward the truth
to embrace it the way a tree grows up reaching into
the light and air and embracing it in an "airy cage"
where light and air move freely.

For St. Augustine the truth is firmly established, ac-
cepted in advance, and he merely contemplates and
explains it in a development of luminous symbols,
and, in fact, there is no logic in any philosophical or
systematic sense about him. He is a preacher, and that
is the best thing to be.

St. Thomas, rather than a preacher, is an apologist
and a philosopher: he is trying to convince the
Gentiles, and has to reduce what Augustine sees to
necessary and systematic terms. He gives Christianity
a sound metaphysical and logical structure which it
needed, as is easily seen when we realise the weakness
of the Protestants is their lack of a metaphysic (this is
truer of Lutherans than of Calvinists).

Historians of philosophy keep talking about the
Augustinian and Thomist traditions in Christian
thought as two radically opposed movements. Ramon
Lull, for example, is an Augustinian. Yet St. Thomas
and St. Augustine are much closer together than St.
Augustine and Lull who, far from being satisfied with
St. Augustine's symbolic theology, is a mathematical

Platonist, and invents countless diagrams and "infallible systems" which prove "everything" with "absolute necessity." Thus this "Augustinian" is really
extremely remote from St. Augustine, having reduced
everything to the logic of mathematics.

¶ There is a new biography of Joyce out which has
confirmed what everybody probably suspected: that
his personal life has been dreary and rather uninter-
esting. I suppose he has been too much whipped. His
pictures show him to be a slight, skinny, small-boned
Irishman; blind, grey, sharpnosed, sharpchinned, a
bit arrogant. One picture showed him in a very stuffy
looking smoking jacket, surrounded by his friends.

He is fastidious looking too. He has long fingers,
small feet. In a lot of ways he reminds me of a missionary I know who has spent the last six years riding
around in the Matto Grosso in the wilderness and heat
bringing the sacraments to Indians.

Joyce certainly looks like an Irishman who resisted
a vocation to the priesthood, but he also looks more
like a bookkeeper than a writer. That he happens to
be the best writer in this century is quite apart from
this, and nobody ever said that his looks had anything

much to do with what he wrote. It is too bad he made the same mistake that the people who hate him have always made: that of making no distinction whatever between the culture of the Irish middle-class and the sacramental life of the Church.

He is always attacking the former, and very rarely the latter: but he makes so little distinction between them that when he makes fun of the Irish middle-class, he leaves it to be clearly understood that he is including everything they might possibly want to believe in.

But to the people who hate him, the middle-class is as sacred as the Mystical Body of Christ and indistinguishable from it, so *everything* he says seems to be blasphemous.

¶ Graham Greene's *Brighton Rock* is good all the way from the quotation on the flyleaf, from "The Witch of Edmonton":

This were a fine reign
To do evil, and not hear of it again.

The book is full of terrific images, witty, complex and metaphysical. He is putting to its very best use a kind of modified surrealism, and the framework of the "thriller" is perfect for what he is trying to do.

I like the song that Ida (a character who thirsts after justice "like the British fleet," but is otherwise the least successful figure in the book) keeps singing over and over in her beery voice: *"One night—in an alley —Lord Rothschild said to me . . ."*

The Boy, the fierce central character is not just a psychological study because, if he were, the book wouldn't have all the meaning it has: the book is a

parable, and you can't quite make parables out of real-
istic, psychological studies. Therefore his fear of sex is
more than just a glib trick of the author in character-
izing him: it carries with it the notion of chastity
turned inside out into a kind of Satanic sterility,
which is a compulsion imprisoning him in evil yet
liberating in him one terrible power: to kill people
swiftly and almost surgically, with complete coldness.
All this is comprehensible in terms of the doctrine of
"corruptio optimi pessima" and the whole thing has
implications that are important for our society which
worships a kind of surgical sterility itself, but cannot
connect up that worship with all the dirt and cruelty
and misery that are forced, harder and harder, upon
the poor.

The best characters in the book are Colleoni and his
gangsters. There is a scene where Colleoni comes
walking grandly through the lobby of a hotel, where
he lives in splendor, followed by a secretary running
behind him and putting down on a pad names of
flowers and fruits which Colleoni calls out as fast as
they come into his head. They are to be sent to C.'s
wife, from whom, of course, he has been separated for
years.

There is another scene, where one of the gangsters,
who is worried sick because he is in danger of being

killed by his own gang, is mooning around on a pier
and gets his character read by a slot machine. The
card comes out in the form of a love letter, not a
fortune. It begins: "Your wondrous winsome beauty
and culture . . ."

Good Friday, 1940

"For in that she hath poured this ointment on my body, she did it for my burial." ST. MATTHEW 26:12.

"He hath delivered His soul unto death." ISAIAS 53:12.

❡ The apostles and, specifically in one Gospel, Judas, complained that this ointment was *wasted* in being poured upon Christ instead of being sold, and the money given to the poor.

Let the people, the so-called Christians who argue against the "imprudence" of certain actions—like, for example, admitting a Negro child to parochial school for fear all the white parents take away their children —remember the "prudence" of Judas.

The Pharisees and Judas gave openly to the poor and to the temple.* There were always prudent folk who knew just how much to give to the poor, and at what season. They knew how to give to the poor so that it wasn't embarrassing, or imprudent, or rash.

* Matthew 6:2; Luke 18:10ff.; John 13:19.

They knew enough not to give the poor so much that they preferred to live on alms and gave up working altogether, the lazy sots. They had a system all worked out, and a lot of special prayers for every penny given away. It was a very efficient system, almost like a modern "Charity" with a huge filing-system and a big sucker-list of names and a lot of little women with glasses hopping around in an office like birds, and a lot more women like mice, scratching at the doors of the poor with notebooks, and asking them their grand-father's birthplace, and do the children have the rickets or the TB, and how much money do the kids make, shining shoes and selling papers? It was perhaps less efficient, but no more human.

The Pharisees knew how to take care of the poor in such a way that the poor would be always with them.

Therefore Christ said to those who objected the ointment should have been sold for the benefit of the poor that, for such gifts, the poor would be always with them.

There is a distinction between Charity, the The-ological Virtue, and Charity a modern word meaning a mechanical and impersonal kind of almsgiving, as, for example, when a millionaire leaves all his money to "Charity." The poor will always be there for this kind of almsgiving, where the rich man, infinitely distant from the poverty of the poor, scratches with a pen on a paper and starts a long series of bookkeeping entries and abstract transactions which end up a long time later with a nervous social worker scolding a group of kids who are trying to play baseball in a crowded street somewhere in a slum.

Without love, almsgiving is no more important an action* than brushing your hair or washing your hands, and the Pharisees had just as elaborate a ritual for those things as they had for giving alms, too, because all these things were prescribed by law, and had to be done and done so. But love does not merely give money, it gives itself. If it gives itself first and a lot of money too, that is all the better. But first it must sacrifice itself.

If everyone had such charity as the woman who wasted, sacrificed this ointment that could have been sold for the poor, the poor would be much better off, and in fact would not be poor at all, or no poorer than anybody else. And what if the ointment had been sold? What about it? What would become of the ointment? What would the next buyer do with it? Pour it on his own head, probably. But because this woman poured out this ointment and "wasted" it all for Christ, her story shall be told until the end of time.

* cf. I Corinthians 13:3.

The perfect Charity of this woman's action is all the nobler when we see how it foreshadows the perfect Charity of Christ's sacrifice for us, which was about to be consummated, as Christ Himself bears witness: "She did it for my burial."

Thus He signalised the perfect Charity of her gift by comparing it to His own passion, which it foretells and illustrates. The preciousness of the ointment testifies to the infinite preciousness of Christ's body and blood, offered up for us on the Holy Cross, a sacrifice that *infinitely* exceeds the object (our souls) which it redeemed.

Yet if the woman had poured out this ointment, not upon God but only upon a prophet, the sacrifice would not have been perfect. And Judas, who did not believe Christ to be the Son of God, was already hardening his heart in stubbornness and suspicion against the words of the One he was about to betray. He thought he was being virtuous, prudent. He was caring for the poor. He was impatient of this crazy, wasteful, imprudent action; it repelled him, and it scared him.

Let the people who are repelled and scared by the Charity of saints, and all who fear those who try to help the poor by giving up everything they have, including their lives, to them, let all these remember the "prudence" of Judas when the woman poured out the ointment, and let them be afraid. Because the woman knew she was in the presence of God, and gave him everything she had while Judas stood by giving a lecture on imprudence, a lecture that was instantly answered and confounded by God Himself.

¶ I saw a Negro workman riding happily on the Long Island train, wearing a woolen cap on his head and reading a Negro newspaper, the Society Page: and down one side of the page he was reading was a great big advertisement reading "Panic Stampede for *Native Son*."

"Panic Stampede" is some phrase! However, I guess it is right, all right. At the bottom of the ad was a coupon you could cut out and send in, so that you would have the book: the idea being that you were a Negro and *Native Son* was by a Negro and naturally you were going to think this was the best book in the world for these reasons.*

---

* I am by no means questioning the talent of Mr. Richard Wright, an important writer who deserves credit for a very respectable achievement. Nor am I trying to deny to Negroes the right to be proud of one of their outstanding authors. The tragic ghetto existence which has been imposed on the Negro race ought to be a reminder that the ghetto mentality is not a good to be embraced, but an evil to be rejected.

37

And then I got very sad, thinking how people who can do so many good things instinctively, like playing pianos and dancing, should have to start imitating the dullest, stupidest tricks of all the crafty, snobbish, petty, absurd little groups that make up the rest of society. I thought of all the socialists walled up in their rooms praising socialist novels, and all the communists growling in their hutches the praises of communist novels, and then I thought of all the Catholics praising the works of some stuffed shirt who happened to be a Catholic, and I thought of the Jews praising novels by Jews, and my mind returned to the polite and soft-voiced and smiling and slightly awkward and intensely earnest Negroes gathered in fairly livable apartments on Edgecombe Avenue, talking about *Native Son,* but not really succeeding in being as stupid as the Communists and the Socialists and the Catholics and the Jews and everybody else. But give them time: they will succeed: they will get to be as dumb as we are.

The terms Communist and Socialist are social classifications. The term Catholic can refer to a social classification or to a religious one, and I am talking about the social one, the way the term is used in conversation. You say so and so is a Catholic. Maybe you just mean he has an Irish name, and was once baptised, and when he blasphemes he blasphemes the

name of Christ without giving the impression at all
that he really knows what he is saying or doing. Or
when you say Catholic, maybe you mean someone who
reads a lot of rather messily got up little magazines
written in bad English and full of sentimental illustrations.* You are still talking about Catholics in the
cultural and not the religious sense.

I heard of a fairly devout Italian woman (I say she
is fairly devout because at least she has a lot of those
awful chromos insulting the Sacred Heart and the
Blessed Virgin on the walls of her apartment) and this
woman read a book called *Black Narcissus* which was
about some kind of a nun falling in love with some
kind of an Indian native. Well, the good woman got
excited and wept a lot and read the book over a couple
of times and for a long time it was her favorite book,
and I wouldn't be surprised if she thought it was a
devotional work.

Then there are all the communists who think
Shakespeare was a kind of a communist, and the Irish
who think Shakespeare was really a man named
O'Neil. And, of course, earnest Catholics (there is
nothing wrong with what they do except that it is
stupid) work hard to try and prove Shakespeare was

* This was written in 1940. I believe U.S. Catholic magazines have
considerably improved since then.

Catholic—and in fact it is quite possible that he was
one, in the end.

Personally I don't care whether Shakespeare's father
was ever signed up by the Jesuits in some under-
ground Catholic club, nor whether Shakespeare was
poaching in the preserves of a "new man" * in order
to get even with him for stealing the house and lands
of a hunted Catholic nobleman and I don't think it
affects the value of *Hamlet* if Shakespeare never went
to mass. Dante didn't fiddle around wondering if Virgil was Catholic (except the Middle Ages were pretty
excited about the Messianic Eclogue's being a prophecy of Christ's coming!) and St. Thomas wasn't trying
to make Aristotle out to be a Christian, nor St. Augustine, Plato.

Truth is truth and whoever beholds the truth sees
God. Catholics did not manufacture the truth, but
truth was given to the Church by God through Christ,
His Word Incarnate, Truth Himself, that we might
come to Him more easily no matter who we are,
peasants or street-sweepers or washwomen or cooks or
firemen or soldiers or kings or writers or priests or
even politicians. But the Church did not create the
truth, and never held any monopoly on that mode of

* i.e., one of the new class that got rich on the spoils of the perse-
cuted Catholics in 16th century England.

it which is accessible to man's natural reason.

You do not have to be a Christian, you have only to know life, to write a play which, like *Hamlet,* is ultimately incomprehensible except in terms of the doctrine of original sin, and illustrates the consequences of it. And if the play is true, it doesn't matter how immoral the hero is, the immorality will appear for what it is, and even more clearly than it would in life. And the play will be moral.

We should stop demanding what the Communists demand of plays and books: that they conform to some abstract set of principles imposed upon them from the outside, not that they should merely tell the truth in their own terms and be good books or plays.

¶ There exists a figure in American literature who is a very interesting sort of a figure, in his own strange way, and that is a man called T. Philip Terry, a writer of guidebooks to Mexico and Cuba. I have just come across him and his imitation Baedekers.

His books are bound like Baedekers and organized like them and printed like them: but there is a difference. Terry has a curious personality which dominates the way his guidebooks are written, and makes them entirely different from Baedekers. Sometimes you wonder whether this personal touch is very desirable: but it is, it makes his guidebooks good and funny.

I can't say I admire his opinions about the Mexicans, whom he continually refers to as "Mex" nor am I happy with his notions of the religious backwardness of these superstitious natives, and I am not totally entranced with his elaborate analogy between the Mexican insult *cabron* ("which is apt to provoke instant physical retaliation") and a "certain inelegant and disparaging accusation (referring to ancestry and moral purity) frequently bandied about by certain American tongues." But anyway it is quite easy to see that this Terry is a wag and a card.

He has a classic little article on Mexican beggars, based on the following concept:

"The average Mex beggar is a chrysalis usually ready to develop into a full-fledged thief." And, he adds, with a relentless and prim severity, "Children are taught to beg from infancy, and though one pities the bedraggled and poorly clad mites, it should be constantly borne in mind that money given them goes directly into the hands of shiftless parents who as promptly spend it for drink."

This is followed by some lofty but practical moralising which explains that the demand for labor in Mexico, at the same time as all this begging continues, far exceeds the supply, and we should neither pity these worthless idlers, nor those "foreign tramps who have no passion for clean linen and make Mexico their winter rendezvous during the season."

The whole article on beggars can be resumed in the following sentence: "There is no lack of charitable organisations in the Republic."

All this is written in the fine spirit of that practical
Yankee morality which long ago put thrift and
prudence at the top of the moral ladder and lowered
"charity" to a word meaning mechanically dispensing
some money to "the poor," in a purely abstract
fashion, relieving the giver from all contact with "the
poor," and incidentally giving the "charitable" organ-
izers a nice cut on the way between the giver and the
far less blessed receiver.

The article on thievery deserves a crown of laurel
more than anything any humanist grammarian ever
wrote in the Italian renaissance!

He begins with the "degenerate Spaniards" who not
only cut their way into houses through the roof, but
rob the poor boxes in the Churches (a temptation
which has since been put out of their way in many of
the provinces of Mexico where the churches are either
destroyed, or else, if open, not allowed to have anything to do with "charity," which has become a function of the government in the more scientific form of
insurance).

This, it is implied, is because of the well known fact
that Christianity has two aspects: one in which it is a
racket practised by the priests, tools of the Capitalists,
on the unsuspecting poor, another where it is a true
ideal, cherished by a few misguided enthusiasts: but

an ideal that is totally absurd and "unscientific." And anyway, the idealists only play right into the hands of scheming clerics!

Terry doesn't get around to expressing such ideas as these, however, but the intellectual descendants of the liberal puritanism he comes from, certainly do.

The important thing is his warning against these rapacious Mexican thieves, these Homeric larcenists: They "steal wire cable by the mile, notwithstanding the risk of electrocution." They take it away and hide it along with "bolts from freight cars, engine fittings . . . lead pipe, bathroom fixtures, potted plants, door plates, push buttons and whatever portable thing can be lifted or wrenched from the house." I like "lifted or wrenched."

As for tourists, they will be more concerned with this warning. Let them beware of ground-floor rooms, even with barred windows, because thieves with "telescopic poles or long canes with hooks at the end" reach in through the grating and fish, indiscriminately for any object in sight.

Speaking of thievery, it has its source: in alcoholic stimulation, he feels.

"The consumers (of *pulque)* are chiefly the idle and common laboring classes to whom it is meat, drink and a constant stimulus to crime."

45

This bourgeois prejudice would have to be erased
from the sentence to describe the present drinkers of
pulque or of Vodka, it would only
be necessary to substitute for "idle and common laboring classes" the words "idle and counterrevolutionary
kulak classes" and that would do the trick.

The similarity of bourgeois prejudices and Communist prejudices is always nearly as striking as the
similarity between bourgeois bad taste in art and
architecture and Communist bad taste in both (in
Russia) which is, if anything, a bit worse.

Both the Communist and the middle-class Puritan
would be very happy about the following splendid
period:

"The zealous but oftentimes bigoted friars, who
ruthlessly destroyed the early Indian manuscripts and
idols, professing to believe them works of the devil lost
no time in replacing them with their own divinities in
wood or plaster, and these, with singular inconsist-
ency, they worshipped with even greater fanaticism."

Brave Terry, noble fellow! Think of those sinful
old bigots committing the crime of destroying *art!*
And being unfair about it too, being *inconsistent,* in
fact singularly inconsistent. Noble satirist! Such
crimes make your Puritan and your Communist weep
with such hot mad tears of outraged justice that they

46

will pick up their hammers and rush blindly to the
nearest Spanish or Russian Church (the job was done
in England and Germany long ago) and start breaking
up the idols there—with singular, of course, consist-
ency!

Immediately after this passage, we are startled by
the change of tone, from bitter but noble satire to
mild and perplexed severity:

"Good music (military) is more often heard in the
Mexican plazas than in churches, where it is of a
purely devotional character."

[Note twenty years later: Today, when relations
between the U.S. and Latin America are considerably
more strained than they were when this was
written, I think it useful to point out that the Terry
mentality is by no means a thing of the past.
Indeed, North American policies in regard to South
America tend sometimes to be unconsciously
saturated with this kind of naive pharisaism. It is
taken for granted that the U.S. is universally benevo-
lent, wise, unselfish and magnanimous in her deal-
ings with Latin American countries. And that the
latter tend to be improvident, wasteful, impractical,
unwise, lazy and even unreliable. It is a very strange
thing to accuse starving workmen of petty thievery
when the economic exploitation of the resources of

their land by foreigners is one of the things that keeps them starving. One is permitted to wonder if the time has not come for the United States to treat Latin America as an equal, and not as a kind of colony that owes us nothing but respect and gratitude, no matter how we behave towards it.]

PART 2

Cuba

[SPRING 1940]

¶ There is a popular superstition about Havana which says that the first thing you see when you approach it on the boat is the Morro Castle. That is not true. I don't know what was the very first thing anyone saw, but the first individual thing on the low shore that got my attention was a big yellow square which turned out to be some building or other in a little village a few miles to the east of Havana.

The next thing was, beyond that, the city itself, the color of a pearl in the morning haze. In the other direction, a low long line of fertile hills stretched along the shore, tapering off eastward into haze and beyond that, suddenly, it led out into a mirage, a second horizon, a second sea hanging low in the sky, and on that sea a small ship steaming north, never seeming to move, just hanging there in the white haze, knocked cockeyed by the reflection of itself, high in

53

the bows and low in the stern and looking something
like a trawler.

Behind the line of low hills, and beyond them was
a line of clouds looking like a fabulous range of jagged
blue mountains, and I had already begun to get the
curious feeling one has about such cloud mountains,
such impossible lovely ranges of mountains, when all
of a sudden as we got closer to shore, it became apparent that these were not cloud mountains at all: but
they were, on the contrary, quite real. Although they
might have been a mirage, they must be the mountains I have read of, that lie north of the town of
Trinidad, in the province of Santa Clara.

Long before you could pick out the Morro at all
(for at that hour in the morning with the sun falling
on it from the shoreward side [to which side it has only
low bastions and earthworks to show] the ramparts
over the harbor mouth were in the shadow) long
before that I had seen the Capitol dome standing
above the city, and could follow the line of white
buildings stretching out along the Malecon toward
The Vedado and beyond.

They were beginning to pile our luggage out on
the narrow and crowded sunny deck, and I walked in
and out among the people, getting, when I could, to
the rail, and looking still over at those hills, thinking

54

of what Columbus said (the words are quoted in any guide, in any travel folder you pick up): "The loveliest land that eyes have ever seen." Although it was lovely land, it was cultivated, and probably is less exciting than it was when Columbus came upon it, all palm trees and flowering jungle. And anyway he landed at the other end of the island.

From out at sea, I don't imagine Havana looks much better than Miami, because Miami from the sea (and only from the sea) looks all right. Havana is a pearl-colored city, you don't know what's going to be in it. From the sea you can't tell.

As you get closer, and begin to enter the harbor, it looks like one of the duller cities along the Mediterranean. There are lines of white and pink and pale orange-colored houses with arcades and archways running along the street. The houses are shuttered, and there is a sea wall, and the place does not appear to be very animated. If you care to, you can look at it as if it were painted in a two dimensional sort of a way on a Dufy screen, throw some bright colors of your own into the picture, and it gets to be fun. But that side of Havana isn't animated. The town gets better when you see the Prado and the parks and the low towers of a church standing here and there not much above the level of the surrounding buildings. Then

Havana suddenly becomes a very charming city: yet
it still isn't particularly animated.

The truth is, you have to leave the dock and get into
the streets before, all of a sudden, the city overwhelms
you, and you are overcome by its brilliance and the
lights and shadows and the noise and the cries and the
colors and the smells and the tremendous vitality that
flows in and out of the big iron gates of the dark
patios, and in and out of the dark shops that stand
open to the street. Then comes the paradox that
Havana in many ways appears to be more of a city
than even New York, because it is a city in the real
sense that Mediterranean and Levantine and perhaps
Oriental cities are cities. There it is not the buildings
that are important but the life in them, and they are
full of life, crammed with it. Negroes with cigars in
their mouths and great bloody aprons, carrying huge
sides of beef out of trucks and into dark cavernous
butcher shops that open right out on the narrow
street. Clusters and clusters of bananas and papayas
and coconuts and God knows what different kinds of
fruits hanging up in the fruiterers'. Piles of cigarettes,
shelves and shelves of books, cigars, medicines, sheets
and sheets of numbered lottery tickets hanging up
over a tobacconist's counter, and more magazines

56

than I ever saw at once in my life: dozens of newspapers.

It is a city that, although it is physically dirty and
full of poor people, is much more a city, and more
truly a rich city than New York because it seems to be
richer in multitudes of material things, fruits, meats,
sugar cane, coffee, tobacco, newspapers, rum, bread,
machinery, musical instruments. New York is only
rich in gold and silver and account books full of
figures and ledgers and fancy printed stocks and ticker
tape and nervous energy and electricity. Havana is
more of a city because it is flesh and blood, bread and
wine, matter charged with life.

It is the nature of a city to be full of people doing
things for some immediate end, commercial, esthetic,
sinful, what you will. They are doing this in a city because each man, there, can supply someone else with
at least one thing he might want. A city is from a
certain point of view a place where proximate satisfaction for almost every order of need or desire is immediately to be had for the asking: you clap your
hands, whistle, beckon to the proper person.

If the nature of a city is such that it makes it possible
for men to satisfy one another's needs directly and
speedily in its streets and market places and its cafés,

it follows that it is better for the city to satisfy needs that already exist and to provide for these well, than for it to *create* artificial needs in order to dispose of new objects, while neglecting to fulfill men's ordinary needs properly. Or, a city that ignores half of men's needs and desires, and concentrates on only one aspect of life, say the commercial, to the exclusion of the esthetic, the moral, etc., is a poor kind of a city.

It is of the nature of a city to attempt to satisfy every class of need. Also, a city where large numbers of people are deprived of even a poor imitation of certain kinds of satisfactions, esthetic or religious or something of the sort, is a failure as cities go, because it is also of the nature of the city to try and provide some sort of satisfaction for everybody's needs.

I can only conclude that a city in which simple needs for everybody are more easily satisfied, in which even the poor have the chance of getting and enjoying more and more of the things that are not essential to base existence, like amusements, etc., and in which more kinds of needs in general are satisfied in more different kinds of ways with less trouble for everybody, that city is better than one where the food is bad for everybody except the rich, where there are only one or two standardised kinds of amusement, where religion is neglected, where more than half the houses are ugly.

Havana is a thoroughly successful city, it is a good city, a real city. There is a profusion of everything in it, immediately accessible, and, to some extent accessible to everybody.

The gaiety of the bars and cafés is not locked in behind doors and vestibules: they are all open wide to the street, and the music and laughter overflow out into the street, and the passersby participate in it, and the cafés also participate in the noise and laughter and gaiety of the street.

That is another characteristic of the Mediterranean type of city: the complete and vital interpenetration of every department of its public and common life. These are cities the real life of which is in the market place, the agora, the bazaar, the arcades.

A Negro, laden down with round red and yellow maracas, and in his hands rattling castanets with a gay sharp roll, circulates in and out the bar, the lobby of the Hotel Plaza: the dining room, which is not separated from the lobby by any dividing wall, shares not only the life and commotion of the lobby but the air the coolness as well as the noise of the arcades outside. You can hear the roll of the castanets as this Negro

goes on out and under the arcades, in and out a bar-
bershop, a café, in between the tall chairs of the boot-
blacks, in and out the pitches of the newsboys with
their hundreds of magazines.

Sellers of lottery tickets, of postcards, or late extra
papers (there is a new edition of some paper almost
every minute) all go in and out of the crowd, in and
out of the bars. Musicians appear under the arcade,
and sing and play and go away again.

If you are eating in the dining room of the Plaza
you share in the life of the whole city. Out through
the arcade you can see, up against the sky, a winged
muse standing tiptoe on top of one of the cupolas of
the National theater. Below that, the trees of the central park: and everybody seems to be circulating all
about you, although they do not literally pass among
the tables where the diners sit, eating dishes savory
with saffron or black beans.

Food is profuse and cheap. As for the rest, if you
don't have the money, you don't have to pay for it: it
is everybody's, it overflows all over the street: Your
gaiety is not private, it belongs to everybody else, because everybody else has given it to you in the first
place. The more you look at the city, and move in it,
the more you love it, and the more love you take from
it, the more you give back to it, and if you want to you

become utterly part of it, of its whole interpenetration of joys and benefits, and this, after all, is the very pattern of eternal life, it is a symbol of salvation, and this sinful city of Havana is so constructed that you may read in it, if you know how to live in it, an analogy of the kingdom of heaven.

I don't know why I had imagined that just because the Cubans speak Spanish it would be fairly easy to get a Spanish edition of the works of St. John of the Cross in Havana. It turned out to be practically impossible: as a matter of fact I still do not know if it is possible at all.

The first day I was in Havana, I was coming up the Calle O'Reilly when I saw a bookstore, a second-hand bookstore, and walked in, asking not for John of the Cross, but for philosophy books. The nearest thing to philosophy on the shelf they pointed out to me were a couple of shabby volumes of literary criticism by Menendez y Pelayo. Then, when I asked for Theology they said they didn't have any.

Another store of the same kind a little further up the street did have a couple of shelves of philosophy: I had to climb a ladder to look at them. I shouldn't have been surprised to be confronted first of all by none other than Nietszche. A little further along, Max

Nordau, whom I take to be some sort of a third rate Spengler. Schopenhauer, Ortega y Gasset: but these are respectable names while, for the most part, the shelves were full of Spanish and French nineteenth-century liberals and radicals of the same sort of calibre as Jaurès. I cannot seem to remember any of the names in particular: but once again, Menendez y Pelayo, too, on literary criticism.

The next place I went into was the Casa Belga with its big stock of French and English books, and its pornography and little editions privately printed in Paris, Henry Miller, Rimbaud's *A Season in Hell* (the salesman took offense when I mentioned that a translation of this had just been published by New Directions in Connecticut: he said this was the original. Not the original original, of course, since it was in English, but the "original translation"). Lots of titles like *The Philosophy of Nudism.* The idea of a philosophy of nudism gave me to laugh somewhat in a quiet scholarly way, to which the salesman refused to grant even a minimum of complicity or assent of any kind. I have always had a certain instinctive respect for the native common sense of the Latin races, who do not indulge in half so many elaborate and sentimental delusions as do teutons, anglo-saxons and celts. For this reason I too readily assumed that this salesman realised right

away that the philosophy of nudism must be an absurd
sort of a book, with a dressed-up pompous title, which
some dope of a tourist would buy for the pictures of
nudists: and so waste his money. But on the other
hand I had forgotten that Cubans and other Latin
Americans are suckers for all kinds of sex books: but
unlike North Americans, they really seem to think
seriously that there exists a philosophy of sex, and
that "sexology" is a science. That is the way the
matter stands, and I can't make up my mind who
are the bigger fools, the Cubans or the North
Americans.

The next place I went to was a bookstore that
looked like a bank and it did not even have books out
on display on the counters: every book in the place
was expensively bound and was locked in behind
wired-in doors. They couldn't help me, either, in my
search for something by St. John of the Cross. Further
down the same street (by now I must have been either
in the Calle Obispo or Obrapia), I did finally come to
a place where they sold books on philosophy.

When I asked for philosophy, they began first to
drag out their John Stuart Mill and Herbert Spencer
and Schopenhauer and so on, but besides that they
had a whole lot of Maritain and Berdyaev in translation, which they brought out very gladly. There I

finally decided to see what Jaime Balmes was like, and took something by him. I immediately regretted it.
The nearest they could get to St. John of the Cross is the autobiography of St. Teresa of Avila, which is such a universal classic that I guess you can get it for thirty cents on the Spanish shelf in Macy's. Anyway, I already have it.

I had given up hunting for St. John of the Cross and was going off up the street when I saw a huge place with a great big sign saying "La Moderna Poesia" which rather astonished me: what a huge shiny big bookstore it was! Only when I looked into one window I saw a lot of straw hats, and in the next a lot of kids suits. It turns out La Moderna Poesia is a department store.

There is also another department store in Havana called "La Filosofia." It would have been funnier if I had run into that one first.

Coming into Havana from the sea the most prominent things on the city skyline besides the Capitol dome (which you see for miles) and the telephone building are the towers of La Reina and Nuestra Senora del Carmen, both big churches. La Reina has a tall gothic spire of pure white stone, the Carmen a square colonial tower with a great statue of the Virgin on top of it. Neither church is in the old section of the city, and both are fairly new. La Reina is quite new, having been finished some time in the twenties. I guess the Carmen is a little older, but not much. Both are very important churches, because they are in populous barrios. La Reina is in a crowded sort of a slum neighborhood in which a great deal of commerce is carried on in cheap, small articles under big and shabby and crowded arcades. The Carmen is in a neighborhood almost as crowded but not quite as poor, and besides, it is near the University and therefore on the edge of the prosperous suburb called the Vedado, which is a very pleasant place full of houses and gardens and shining four or five story modernistic apartments.

The good thing about these neighborhoods, which are both about a mile from the Parque Central, is that tourists do not frequent them, and consequently neither do the pimps, guides, sellers of French postcards and so on. I found out it was an easy way to escape from all that, to get on a bus and ride with it until I got in the clear. Then I could get down again and walk about the streets and arcades, among the people, with no one to bother me.

The Gothic interior of La Reina is tremendous, dark and rather cold. Every man to his own taste, but

I myself have never been particularly fond of the
Gothic revival. As Gothic revival goes, I suppose La
Reina is a pretty good job. I like the tower all right.

The sanctuary is a jumble of precious tropical
woods and stones and metals carved out into symbols
of the faith which I could not disentangle and all cen-
tering around a tremendous Christ. The whole thing
was carved by Catalans and shipped over to Cuba to
be put together.

This was the first Church I went into in Havana.
Aesthetically I am not particularly fond of it, but
nevertheless the place is impressive, and its impressiveness testifies to something of great importance. It
strikes the person coming into it with great force,
overwhelms him and fills him with a kind of awe so
that at least the artist managed to communicate a sense
of the power and majesty of God. But what is more important, that sense of awe is not adventitious or facile:
it is something deep and unforgettable because this
church communicates a true sense of the reality of
God's power as something that moves with deep might
in the most secret place of every person's self. I can
imagine people who don't believe in God being scared
to death by La Reina, and not knowing by what, but
if they went out angry because of that and concluded
the Jesuits had designed the place out of malice with

the intention of scaring comfortable and sensible materialists they would be all wrong. The impressiveness of La Reina, and the way it awes you with a sense of the reality of God's power, form only one aspect of the sense of reality of God that the Spanish possess to a greater degree than most other people. The example of it that anglo-saxons are fondest of exclaiming against is the intense reality with which the suffering of the Crucified Christ can be expressed in the religious art of Spain.

For "liberal" and non-Catholic religious thought, the crucifixion soon became a very different thing from what it has always been for Catholics. To begin with, the terrible sorrow of the Stabat Mater Dolorosa is taken away, although there is an increased stress, a return of emphasis upon the two thieves. Then the Crucifixion itself becomes bloodless, and insensibly the emphasis is shifted from Calvary back to the Palace of Pontius Pilate, and to the Trial, and soon one begins to wonder about the reasons for the condemnation of Christ. One turns to the study of how He happened to get condemned, and away from the fact of His Crucifixion. The reasons for the condemnation of Christ were foolish and He Himself was, of course, innocent. But then we begin to tell ourselves, of course, it was true He was innocent: but it is quite natural that, with the set of interests there were, that needed to have Him out of the way, He got condemned: as if the interests of a couple of tribes in one of the second-rate provinces of the Roman Empire had some importance of their own! The next step is easy; we proceed from examining the reasons why Christ got condemned to reflecting upon the fact that, after all, Pontius Pilate wasn't such a bad fellow: he was a gentleman, a cultivated Roman, and he *saw* that Christ was innocent, didn't he? Well, we too see that Christ was innocent, and by now we have come to delude ourselves that this was all that counted. He was innocent, but then, what can you do? He had all the powerful and rich Jews against him, and everybody knows you can't defend yourself if the moneyed interests are out to get you. As long as you recognise the truth, that He was innocent, that is all that is necessary, let Him die!

But why should He die? Well, that is an uncomfortable sort of a thing to talk about. Perhaps no one knows. But anyway, it is obvious that is the only fitting end to a dramatic story. Imagine if He had lived to a good old age, surrounded by disciples, He would have made no more popular impression on the world than some old Greek philosopher. The question of the

Love of Christ is of course in horrid taste, and nobody would dare mention it.

So, finally, your good comfortable anglo-saxon materialist comes to recognise that Pontius Pilate was really a pretty good sort. Pilate was in a ticklish position, and he got out of it after doing his best to compromise. In the end he did a rather sporting thing. He recognised that Christ was innocent and washed his hands of the whole affair. Pontius Pilate is the hero of the nineteenth century. He was a great liberal.

When the story of the Crucifixion has reached such a state of distortion that its hero has become Pilate and not Christ, then naturally the blood, which Pilate tried to wash off of his hands, must not come into it at all. Calvary remains out of sight, and is not talked about. It must, if possible, be kept in the background lest by chance the prophecy be fulfilled "they shall look upon Him whom they pierced." Remember, we have tried to wash our hands of His blood; we have recognised Him to be without guilt. Now let us alone, will you?

When we try to pretend there was no blood at the Crucifixion, it means not that we are humane, not that we detest sadism and the thought of cruelty, not that we are so gentle and loving in our hearts that we

cannot bear the sight of bloodshed, not that we are
peacemakers who would turn away from the very
thought, the very picture of the spilling of blood:
those excuses are all lies, and all they mean is that we,
like Pilate, are ready to acquiesce in the betrayal of
Christ to spare ourselves trouble or pain or discomfort.

When we try to pretend that there was no blood at
the Crucifixion it means we are trying, like Pilate, to
wash our hands of that blood. That is why we secretly
approve of Pilate; he did what we would have done.
But before Pilate's hands were dry, the Jews had laid
the heavy cross upon Christ's shoulder and were driving him up the path to Calvary. That morning He had
been scourged, and He still wore a crown of thorns;
He fell three times upon the road. They drove nails in
His hands and feet and when He was dead, the soldiers pierced His side with a spear. "And then came
there forth blood and water."

The Spanish know very well that this was so, and
the Crucifixions in their churches show it. The hands
and feet and side of Christ are bloody: and generally
the knees too, because they have not forgotten that
He fell three times, carrying the cross. That they have
such a real sense of the sufferings of Christ brings
upon the Spanish accusations of cruelty, and it is
pointed out that they also like bull-fights and cock-

fights, and that they are cruel to animals and that they
are hot-blooded and violent, and their arguments end
in stabbings and they fight civil wars, hold inquisi-
tions. Sometimes it is said the keenness with which
they feel the sufferings of Christ is a sort of root cause
of the rest of this "Spanish cruelty," sometimes that
both proceed from one cause, but in any case there
is an "inevitable connection" between this barbarous
cruelty and the bloodiness of Spanish crucifixes. The
Spaniards would do well, it is invariably suggested, to
forget about the sufferings of Christ and they might
turn out more "humane." Well, the English are humane and love animals all right, but there is more
than one kind of cruelty. There is a certain kind of
beastly, ice-cold English spite that goes on and on and
on until it blasts and withers everything within its
reach, and is as terrible a thing as any murder, and
just as often ends in murder as do sudden Spanish
bursts of anger. The worst of this spite, too, is that it
is relentless, and never alternates with any kind of
love, as sudden anger does. But then, does the brutality of German concentration camps arise out of some
necessary connection with meditation upon the sufferings of Christ? Or the cruelty of Turks, or Chinese,
or Japanese, or Mohammedans, or Soviet secret police-
men, or of lynch mobs in the southern states of Amer-

ica or other parts of the country? There is so much
violence and cruelty everywhere in the world that no
conclusions one may want to draw about the connection of Spanish crucifixions with Spanish "cruelty"
mean anything at all.

The truth is that at the same time as possessing a
keen sense of the reality of the suffering of Christ on
the cross, they have just as keen a sense of the power
and justice of Christ the King, and just as keen a sense
of the reality of His infinite Love and Mercy for us,
and of the reality of the love of the Blessed Virgin has
for us too, and the saints, and the angels. It is absurd
to talk statistics in a case like this: but let me point out
the obvious thing that nine-tenths of all the statues in
any Spanish church are statues of saints and of the
Virgin or of the Sacred Heart or of the Christ Child,
all of which display a sense of the reality and immen-
sity of His love, and not merely of the intense suffering
He bore on account of that love.

Nuestra Senora del Carmen is a big triumphant
church, with wide arches and baroque ornament and
plenty of light: and the reredos behind the High Altar
is particularly fine. In the middle of it is the Virgin of
Mount Carmel, triumphant, beautiful, merciful,
wearing a crown and carrying the Christ Child, the
King, Her Son. On one side is St. John of the Cross,

carrying of course a cross and looking up directly into the light of heaven. On the other side is St. Teresa of Avila, enraptured, with the dove, symbol of the Holy Spirit, flying above her. On Sundays the Carmen is crowded to the doors all morning, like all the other churches in Havana. Girls with black lace mantillas covering their heads, and men and children, and among them an astonishingly big proportion of beautiful people, beautiful eyes and faces, beautiful gestures, people full of joy and kindness and grace. That is the same everywhere, in every church: El Santo Cristo, La Merced, San Francisco, or the Cathedral of San Cristobal de la Habana.

¶ The complete interpenetration of every department of public life in Cuba, the overflowing of the activities of the streets into the cafes and the sharing of the gaiety of restaurants by the people in the arcades outside, also applies to Churches. There, the doors being open, while Mass is going on you unfortunately get all the noise and activity of the street outside going on too: the clanging of the trolleycar bells, the horns of the buses and the loud cries of the newsboys and the sellers of lottery tickets. Outside the church of St. Francis, the Sunday I was there, a seller of lottery tickets was going up and down and shouting out his special number with the loudest and strongest voice in the whole of Cuba, and Cuba is a country of loud voices. It was a fine sounding number, four thousand four hundred and four:

Cuatro mil cuatro cientos CUA-TRO,
Cuatro mil cuatro cientos CUA-TRO!

74

And so he went on, adding some half intelligible yell now and then that had something to do with Saint Francis—probably that St. Francis liked the number too. *"Cuatro mil cuatro cientos CUA-TRO!"* You could hardly hear the communion bell.

All that is, perhaps, unfortunate. It is a shame that a lot of noise from the streets should fill churches during the consecration, but after all, a person who is really following the Mass is not distracted by it, and forgets about it soon enough.

As I came in the front door of San Francisco, a crowd of children, from the school I suppose, filed in one of the side doors two by two and began taking their places in the front of the church until gradually the first five or six rows were filled. Mass had already begun, and the priest was reading the epistle. Then a brother in a brown robe came out, and you could see he was going to lead the children in singing a hymn. High up behind the altar St. Francis raised his arms up to God, showing the stigmata in his hands; the children began to sing. Their voices were very clear, they sang loud, their song soared straight up into the roof with a strong and direct flight and filled the whole church with its clarity. Then when the song was done, and the warning bell for consecration chimed in with the last notes of the hymn and the church filled

75

with the vast rumour of people going down on their knees everywhere in it: and then the priest seemed to be standing in the exact center of the universe. The bell rang again, three times.

Before any head was raised again the clear cry of the brother in the brown robe cut through the silence with the words "Yo Creo . . ." "I believe" which immediately all the children took up after him with such loud and strong and clear voices, and such unanimity and such meaning and such fervor that something went off inside me like a thunderclap and without seeing anything or apprehending anything extraordinary through any of my senses (my eyes were open on only precisely what was there, the church), I knew with the most absolute and unquestionable certainty that before me, between me and the altar, somewhere in the center of the church, up in the air (or any other place because in no place), but directly before my eyes, or directly present to some apprehension or other of mine which was above that of the senses, was at the same time God in all His essence, all His power, all His glory, and God in Himself and God surrounded by the radiant faces of the uncountable thousands upon thousands of saints contemplating His glory and praising His Holy Name. And so the unshakable certainty, the clear and immediate knowledge that heaven was right in front of me, struck me like a thunderbolt and went through me like a flash of lightning and seemed to lift me clean up off the earth.

To say that this was the experience of some kind of certainty is to place it as it were in the order of knowledge, but it was not just the apprehension of a reality, of a truth, but at the same time and equally a strong movement of delight, great delight, like a great shout of joy and in other words it was as much an experience of loving as of knowing something, and in it love and knowledge were completely inseparable. All this was caused directly by the great mercy and kindness of God when I heard the voices of the children cry out "I believe" in front of the altar of St. Francis. It was not due to anything I had done for my part, or due to any particular virtue in me at all, but only to the kindness of God manifesting itself in the Faith of all those children. Besides it was in no way an extraordinary kind of experience, but only one that had greater intensity than I had experienced before. The certitude of faith was the same kind of certitude that millions of Catholics and Jews and Hindus and everybody that believes in God have felt much more surely and more often than I, and the feeling of joy was the same kind of gladness that everybody who has ever loved anybody or anything has felt. There is nothing esoteric about such things, and I am sure they happen to absolutely everybody, in some degree or other.

These movements of God's grace are peculiar to nobody, but surely they stir in everybody, for it is by them that God calls people to Him, and He calls everybody. Therefore they do not indicate any particular virtue or any special kind of quality. They are common to every creature that was ever born with a soul. But we tend to destroy their effects, and bury them under our own sins and selfishness and pride and lust so that we feel them less and less. And when we do get struck with a strong movement of God's grace, if He means to be particularly merciful, it shows us all the horror of our sins more clearly than we ever saw them before, by comparison with the effects of this mercy. The unhappiness of our sins shows up with all the more ugliness compared with the beauty of the joy we feel for one instant by God's grace.

¶ I suppose Cuba is too poor for a false feast like Mother's Day to be much of a commercial success, and for that reason Mother's Day has actually taken hold in Cuba. It is really something of a genuine feast, and it is certainly a religious one. It got mentioned from the pulpit, and you could see that it meant something to everybody, too. Mother's Day is really a success in Cuba, a success which it can never hope to be in the U.S., precisely because in Cuba it is useless to try and make it into a big advertising gag for candy and small presents, since not everybody here can afford that sort of thing.

Instead of that, everybody goes to church and everybody wears a flower in his buttonhole, a red rose if his mother is living and a white one if she is dead, the red and white each having a meaning which was explained from the pulpit in the church of San Francisco. So you see everybody walking about loving their mothers, while in America the sale of candy and the amount of talk about loving one's mother is out of all proportion to the actual love that is shared between mothers and their children. On top of that comes this great commercial insult, and so many other things of the same kind, that anyone with a grain of sensibility or decent feeling begins to wonder whether the love of one's mother is not a false and shameful thing if it lends itself, without any protest, to exploitation by charlatans. One immediately wonders why, if Americans really do love their mothers, they should tolerate for an instant that their love should become the object of so great a buffoonery. I do not insist that millions of perfectly happy North Americans cannot love their mothers and go on loving them without being corrupted by Mother's Day, and even giving Mother's Day presents out of love and not out of compulsion or false emotion. But all that does not apply to Cuba. And probably if the truth is known they do really love their mothers in Cuba, and that is why Mother's Day is a commercial failure there, but at the same time a great moral success.

This is not to say that there is not as much sentimentality about motherhood in Cuba as there is in America, but even then, the sentimentality in Cuba is rather more sound, and fundamentally closer to a

more important kind of truth about motherhood.
Take the front pages of the *Havana Post* and *El Pais*
on Mother's Day, 1940. Of course most of the page is
taken up by the German invasion of Belgium and
Holland, a thing which demonstrates clearly that Hitler is diabolically inspired, is making war for its own
sake, not even for the sake of conquest, but as an end
in itself, his purpose being not to beat England and
France without getting America in it, but on the contrary, to get the whole world in the war again, to make
sure the thing is really universal. Germany's defeat
does not matter, because he will then have ensured
the destruction of the whole earth besides; it is a fundamentally diabolical instinct for mass suicide. However, to get back to Mother's Day. The Dutch news
cannot keep from the front page a certain tribute to
motherhood: and it took typical forms in one paper
and the other. In the *Havana Post* (the local American
paper) it was of course the silver-haired old lady, sitting hunched up in a chair in a foggy, blurred sort of
atmosphere so that you could not clearly see any of
her features. That is the usual North American
version. Mother is wrinkled and frail but brave
enough to bake an apple pie at the drop of a hat,
and what America is really talking about all the
time is grandmotherhood. Cuba, on the other hand,

is not. That is what makes Cuban Mother's Day one stage less remote from the truth than the North American Mother's Day. I therefore propound this rule:

Rule: When the Cubans talk about Mother's Day, and the love of mothers, they really mean mothers and not grandmothers: and also they really mean love, and not presents.

This is a good thing.

Therefore the picture on the front of *El Pais* was under a headline saying: *"Las Madres, fuente de la vida"* or mothers the fountain of life, and showed a picture of a young mother with a lot of children around her, a very clear picture of a mother and her children all happy and smiling and having their arms around each other. Not a wrinkled up sweet old lady with no children, but mothers in as much as they are mothers, the source of life, not fountains of cookies and brownies and inexhaustible supplies of apple pie such as Cushman cannot hope to imitate. The sentimental reverence for fountains of life can also unquestionably be overdone, but it is so much harder to overdo something that after all has such a real importance! Life is one thing and apple pie quite another.

¶ The *Teatro Principal* held three surprises for me in
Camaguey. The first one was, that the lights suddenly
went up, after the movie was over, and I discovered
that the audience was full of white suits and pretty
dresses, and that, therefore, my dismal apprehension
that the town was falling to pieces and dying of starvation had been an illusion produced by the lack of
electric light in the narrow and silent streets. The
third was that I discovered, from the top of the tower
of *La Merced,* that this theater was a huge whale-
backed place, one of the biggest buildings in town.
The second was the most agreeable: the Mexican
vaudeville troupe of Beatriz Nolesca.

"Beatriz Nolesca," (said the signs), "bailes, arte,
juventud." Dances, art, youth. What came on first was
not youth but a middle-aged Mexican Panurge, and I
began immediately to laugh myself silly because I
could just barely understand all his jokes, so that the

pleasure at being able to understand them combined with the mediocre pleasure implicit in the jokes themselves to make them sound really humorous. But he was a good guy, and looked like a Marseillais, and his humor was the rhetorical *miles gloriosus* stuff the Marseillais make much of. Maybe I should not apologise for laughing.

He made a short speech. Then came three Mexican girls that looked like kitchen maids in everything, attitude, clothes, gestures and all, and did a dance with some earthenware plates and some Mexican music. My curiosity about Mexico began to diminish rapidly, and yet I was gaga, fascinated by this dance. This was my first night in this strange town in this strange country and I did not yet know what to make of the place or any experience that occurred in it. I was open-mouthed, like a cowboy in off the plain to see this same show, and I didn't lose a gesture of the dance.

I will never forget it as long as I live, it was so bad, it was so beautiful. Plates on one side, plates on the other side, they swing their heads to this side, to that side, sway, turn, plates here, plates there, smiling all the time. Tan tan tan, tan tan tan: the sort of music all tin strings that ought to have a marimba to it also! This way, that way.

One girl was round-faced, the other was really fat,

the third was slim and had slim legs and a sort of a cat-like face that was mean and pretty, and she knew she was more graceful than the others. Without there having been much clapping at all, they did a whole encore, the whole thing all over, just as a matter of routine, as if they *had* to do it twice. It was so pretty and so awful: this side, that side, turn, sway. Tan tan tan; tan tan tan. At the end they twirl around and up go their skirts like light bells around their up-on-tiptoe legs. Ding Ding. The end.

They run awkwardly off the stage. I never saw anything so lousy or so unforgettable or so fascinating. It wasn't that they danced badly. They danced very well a dance that was so bad it made you want to cry, so bad, so meaningless. Some Mexicans!

It was even worse when the plump one came running out in a tight black short-coated furry man's Mexican cowboy outfit, so black and tight and furry it made her look like a huge mouse, and all her movements were indeed those of a giant mouse, and that was what her smile wrote all over her face: "Now you may see that I am the giant mouse."

This number was really more awful than the other, and with no good dancing to compensate for the badness of the whole conception. I was transfixed by this dance: when it was over I could have wept.

Really the funny scenes were good. One of the sketches is about a machine for rejuvenating old men. The machine belongs to the owner of a beauty parlor and to this Panurge of a janitor who has been given half a share in it for back wages. An old woman and a young girl come in to have the girl's ninety-five-year-old fiance reduced to a decent age: she wants him twenty, the mother wants him thirty. The Panurge, after a lot of explaining about how the machine works, goes off, and comes back driving and whipping and kicking the old man across the stage and off the other side to where the machine is. You know that the machine rings a bell every time the man in it has lost five years. The bells start, count off some sixty years, and then start going furiously ding ding ding ding ding, while Panurge comes dashing back saying he can't find the switch, can't find the key to get the old man out, etc., etc. Another interpretation of Huxley's problem! Nothing is left of the old man but his black suit and hat. The reason for this is that the old man was the giant mouse dressed up in another costume. Or maybe the giant mouse was the daughter: I think not.

There was another sketch about a birthday party. The giant mouse had a birthday party. The sketch wasn't funny, but the business in it was. A girl comes in with a great white dog under her arm and hands it to the other girl as a present. The dog is really just a little too big to be handed around, and it is funny. Then they say the dog's name is "Como tu" (like you) and they work that gag until it dies of exhaustion, then the dog barks and runs around and raises a lot of fuss and goes off. The real part of the sketch is to do with Panurge, all gallant and important bowing and larfing and guzzling all the beer and dancing with all the ladies, each lady in turn fainting with great screams because she is overpowered by his body odor. All the dancing and fainting is very funny.

I went to see them again the second night, in a different bill, but they were not so good at all: there was something strangely disturbing in seeing those same gestures all over again even in different contexts. Both times, however, the giant mouse managed to be a giant mouse and both times, after a dance by two girls (again with a plate, which one of them dropped, on the second night), Panurge came out and held up his hands to still the dying applause crying:

"*Muchisimas gracias, respetable publico, son mis hermanas las dos.*—Thank you, thank you, respectable public: they are my sisters, both of them!"

¶ Our modern rat-race civilisation, having lost, at the same time, its respect for virginity and for fruitfulness, has replaced the virtue of chastity with a kind of hypochondriac reverence for perfect, sterile cleanliness: everything has to be wrapped in cellophane. Your reefers come to you untouched by human hands. Fruitfulness has lost its meaning but has degenerated into a kind of sentimental and idolatrous worship of sensation for its own sake that is so dull it makes you vomit: the fat blondes in the dirty picture magazines are getting bigger and fatter and more rubbery, and all the people who think they are so lusty are really worshipping frustration and barrenness. No wonder they go nuts and jump out of windows all the time. Such contradictions are completely unbearable, and cannot be replaced by a lot of mental and sexual gymnastics, the way the mental cripples who have been psychoanalysed seem humbly to believe.

There is more talk about Peace, Life and Fertility now than at any other time in the history of the world, especially, of course, in Germany and Italy. (The Italian Fascists all talk like shrivelled up old men, mumbling between their gums, "Life, Life, Youth!") At the same time the people who yell loudest about all these things are clearly responsible for the worst war that was ever heard of, and are also busy putting out of existence in lethal chambers everybody that has gone crazy as a result of this kind of thinking (gone crazy, that is, without getting into the government).

¶ Last night I was scared right out of a movie by an English picture that was so vile I was momentarily convinced England is done for forever. Although the picture has nothing to do with war, it is such a failure that it makes it totally comprehensible that the English should have failed in everything else they have undertaken in the political sphere also. It was Merle Oberon in "Over the Moon."

Underneath the chirping, surface gaiety and self-possessing of the lines (I have nothing against Merle Oberon) is the inhuman frigid cheapness of *Tit Bits, Pantomime Choruses* and all kinds of poor, frozen Cockney bravery that it all cries out for vengeance because it was produced by the grinding materialism of the worst industrial slum-civilisation that has ever yet been seen on the face of the earth. It is the cheerfulness of a people that have had all the life ground out

of them, and are dead beat except for this heart-rend-
ing and useless bird-talk bravery! Those pitiful stiff
upper lips and toothless smiles of the English working
class!

PART 3

New York and St. Bonaventure

[1940–1941]

¶ The room I had in Havana, in the cheap hotel up by
the University, had a hard bed which frequently col-
lapsed. It was on a corner of the building and one window opened towards the fake Columbia of the university, the other towards the Calle San Lazaro. Through
that other came the reflection of the tower of Nuestra
Senora del Carmen, and the great statute of the
Blessed Virgin was caught in the mirror of my ward-
robe, and I could look at it when I woke up in the
bed, reflected there, with the sky behind it unusually
white in the glass.

I have been cleaning my stuff out of a room I had
on Perry Street. I lived in it all winter, sitting at the
desk, spending more time in it than in any other room
I ever lived in, for the same period of time.

What was I doing?

Going through the *Spiritual Exercises* of St. Ignatius.

Correcting papers written by my English Class in Columbia night school: "My Favorite Movie Star." "Is It Possible To Be Happy Without Money?"

Lying on the bed with five or six stitches in my jaw where a wisdom tooth had been torn and hammered from the bone: the sweet smell of Gilbert's antiseptic filled the whole place for weeks afterward. As a consolation, I feebly turned over and over the pages of travel folders about Mexico, Cuba, Brazil. (I knew all along I would only be able to afford Cuba.)

Most of the time I wrote and wrote: This Journal, long-hand, in a ledger. A novel that has perplexed three publishers without any result. And also I read. Pascal; the *Little Flowers* and *Rule* of St. Francis; Lorca; Rilke; *The Imitation of Christ;* St. John of the Cross and also William Saroyan, when I was too tired to read the hard stuff.

¶ It is said that while the Germans were desecrating a church somewhere in Poland, some German sergeant, cockeyed with the excitement, stood up in front of the altar and yelled out that if there was a God He would want to prove His existence at once by striking down such a bold and important and terrifying fellow as this sergeant. God did not strike him down. The sergeant went away still excited, and probably the unhappiest man in the world: God had not acted like a Nazi. God was not, in fact, a Nazi, and God's justice (which everybody obscurely knows about in his bones, no matter what he tries to say he thinks) is inexpressibly different from the petty bloodthirsty revenge of Nazis.

God, according to His inscrutable will, does occasionally strike such fools down: but who was struck down at the crucifixion of Christ? Christ's passion and resurrection are greater than any imaginable miracle,

the transubstantiation of the bread and wine into the
Body and Blood of Christ is far more miraculous than
God's striking down somebody who desecrates the
Blessed Sacrament: it is a far greater and more terri-
fying thing that Christ in the Sacrament should *sub-
mit* to desecration.

Nobody was struck down on Calvary. The heavens
split and the veil of the temple was rent and the earth
shook, but all for those of us who are weak in faith,
and who of us isn't? But who was struck down? The
Pharisees? Was Judas blasted by lightning or did he go
and hang *himself?*

The most terrifying thing that happened on Calvary was not that the earth was shaken to its founda-
tions, but that the Son of God cried out: "My God,
my God, why hast Thou forsaken Me!"

May 26, 1940

¶ And if we go into the war, it will be first of all to defend our investments, our business, our money. In certain terms it may be useful to defend all these things, and expedient to protect our business so that everybody may have jobs, but if anybody holds up American business as a shining example of justice, or American politics as a shining example of honesty and purity, that is really quite a joke!

And if this is a joke, it is also a bit blasphemous to get up and say that just because Germany started the actual fighting, ultimately Germany is to blame for everything, and God is on the side of England and the democracies and all enemies of Germany.

To try to make God the defender of any one side in this war is simply to reduce Him to the level of a Nazi, and no greater blasphemy is possible. But, besides that, it is irrational to the point of lunacy. We know the Nazis half expect, from moment to moment, to be struck down by fire from heaven, because they have an ineradicable suspicion that there is a God somewhere, and if there is one, He must be like a Nazi, and ready to destroy even His friends at the first sign of anything that displeases Him.

The tragedy is that the English and Americans and all the others are also disappointed because God is not a Nazi. Because if God were a Nazi, at the first false step of the Germans, their entry into Czechoslovakia, He would have blasted them into atoms for violation of an agreement.

If God allows the Nazis to attack England, and even destroy her, it is precisely because He is not a Nazi. As soon as we forget that God's justice is not the justice of a tough, erratic and rather venal police sergeant, but that it is identified with His love, we become incapable of understanding anything about God, because we are thinking no longer of Christ, but of Thor, or Odin.

The justice of a barbarian deity is not in the least inscrutable, although it may be a little crazy at times: you do something that offends him, and he breaks your neck. But the Justice and Love of a God who dies for those who offend Him, on a cross, the death of a slave, is totally inscrutable, and is to be adored and imitated before it can be understood, because it can only be understood when it has been to some extent imitated and loved.

But if God *were* just only in the sense that a cop is just—that is, you offend against his book of rules, and he arrests you—then instantly he would strike us all down for the very blasphemy of comparing him to an ordinary human policeman!

If God were a stormtrooper, there wouldn't be a single stormtrooper left in Germany. Berlin would be ashes. Instead, some, not all, of the churches in Poland are ashes.

However, to say that God is punishing the Church is far worse than imagining that he ought, right now, at our wish, to punish the Nazis. God does not punish the Church: He punishes sinners—and how He does we cannot very well conceive. Wars, plagues, famines have something to do with His punishment, not so much because they are the punishment itself, but because they are warnings of the eternal punishment to come. Christ said of all these things:

"It shall happen to you for a testimony" (St. Luke, xxi, 13) and St. Gregory the Great makes the comment that all these tribulations merely point to the Last Judgment and the tribulations in eternity for those who never consent to love God, but willingly cut themselves off from Him.

"Ultima tribulatio multis tribulationibus prevenitur; et per crebra mala quae preveniunt, indicantur mala perpetua quae subsequentur." *

It is conceivable, for instance, that God's punishment of the earth should operate in some strange manner in which those who hate Him are allowed to torture and kill those who love Him and whom He loves: that is, the poor, and the holy. For, in this, the Crucifixion of Christ is re-enacted, because when He was crucified, He even bore the punishment and the suffering of those who murdered Him! He even bore the punishment of Judas, if Judas himself had willed to ask for forgiveness: but even after the betrayal, Judas was damned by his own despair, and therefore took the punishment upon himself.

It is even conceivable that God should let the whole Church suffer crucifixion as the world's "punishment" before the last day—that is, He might let the world crucify the Church, and the Church suffer in this crucifixion once again for the salvation of the world.

For Christ suffers in the Church: and there is nothing suffered on earth that Christ Himself does

* "The final tribulation is preceded by many tribulations; and, by the frequent evils which go before, are shown the perpetual evils which are to follow."

not suffer. Everything that happens to the poor, the meek, the desolate, the mourners, the despised, happens to Christ.

The only thing that can save us is an army of saints—and not necessarily Joan of Arcs, or military saints. Where will they come from? Nobody can really say, except those who think about it seem to believe (like Maritain) the saints will come from the poorest of the laity, from the depths of the slums, from the concentration camps and the prisons, from the places where people are starving, bombed, machine-gunned and beaten to death. Because, in all these places, Christ suffers most. Maritain adds, I remember, that they will also be found in religious orders—especially the contemplative ones.

And the rest of us, what should we do? Fall down and pray and pray over and over to God to send us saints!

¶ I was reading a Paris Letter in a copy of *Partisan Review,* maybe a year old. It dealt with a whole lot of personalities and issues nobody had ever heard of except that the writer stopped to sneer at Cocteau's *Parents Terribles,* which I haven't read. He covered himself up with elaborate protestations that he wasn't criticising Cocteau on moral grounds, indicating that he knew the argument that says a work of art should be judged in its own terms, and then went ahead and criticised the play on political grounds, which is an even worse mistake. He never got around to talking about the play in its own terms at all. Which all goes to show that the people on *Partisan Review* have read a little more than the ones on *New Masses,* and know what is good taste and what is intellectually fashionable, and write a little more subtly, and yet make just as big mistakes, if not bigger ones, all the time.

But the most interesting thing in the letter was some grief over the fact that some idiot French Fascist had mutilated a statue by Epstein. Epstein must think by now that he is a very important artist, the way people make demonstrations over his statues.

But there you are. Epstein is a Jew. Nazis hate Jews. Communists hate Nazis. Nazis hate Epstein, therefore Communists (for the time being) love Epstein because the Nazis hate him. French Fascists hate Communists, Jews, Epstein, and particularly Epstein's latest statue, which French Communists are thereby furiously prompted to love. If either side ran across the statue in a warehouse, with no label on it, and if they had absolutely no means of knowing who had made the thing, they probably wouldn't know whether they liked it or not. They would remain speechless. They wouldn't have a judgment.

This is called the Proletarian Theory of Art.

When the Fascists mutilated that statue, the Communists screamed as if it was their own flesh. They explained their scream as the evidence of their horror at seeing art so despised and desecrated. However, if it happened to be the best picture of the year, but was signed Giorgio di Chirico, and somebody threw a brick through it, then your Communists would remain miraculously calm in the presence of something unpleasant happening to a work of art. In fact, you would probably find that one of them had thrown the brick.

And, as a matter of fact, this same letter that laments the mutilation of the Epstein statue gloats over the fact that Chirico is supposed to be in trouble in Rome, with his bosses. They are just crazy about art, those boys! They judge it on its own terms!

And yet the *Partisan Review* is at least an important magazine: it is one of the only ones left in the country that, with all its mistakes, at least has something to say.

¶ The French have been driven south to the Loire;
Lax, Rice and Gibney have gone to the lake, and I
am sitting by myself in the middle of the driveway
outside the cottage, looking at the woods.

Just because nobody I ever knew wanted a war, I
imagined the Germans didn't either, and all the time
they wanted nothing else. No, not all of them. But
you hear of the tremendous enthusiasm of some of
the German troops in this fight: they like it, and that
is why they are winning. Nobody else likes war.

Here it is very quiet and sunny. In front of me
there is a bush covered with pale white blossoms that
do not smell of anything much. Somewhere under
some thorns and weeds a cricket sings drily. Everything is quiet and sunny and good, but I am tempted
to make no sentimental comparisons between this
and the valley of the Loire.

It is possible to imagine a man coming silently out

of these woods into the open grass space before me
and aiming a gun and shooting me dead in this
chair, and going away again.

Even though there is sunlight, the woods might
well fill, all at once, with the clack and roar of tanks.
The aeroplane that went by an hour ago might have
been filled with bombs, but it just wasn't. There is
nothing too fantastic to believe any more, because
everything is fantastic. There is no fighting here
now, but there could very well be plenty tomorrow.

The valley is full of oil storage tanks, and oil is for
feeding bombers, and once they are fed they have to
bomb something, and they generally pick on oil
tanks.

Wherever you have oil tanks, or factories, or rail-
roads or any of the comforts of home and manifesta-
tions of progress, in this century, you are sure to get
bombers, sooner or later.

Therefore, if I don't pretend, like other people, to
understand the war, I do know this much: that the
knowledge of what is going on only makes it seem
desperately important to be voluntarily poor, to get
rid of all possessions this instant. I am scared, sometimes, to own anything, even a name, let alone coin,
or shares in the oil, the munitions, the airplane fac-

tories. I am scared to take a proprietary interest in anything, for fear that my love of what I own may be killing somebody somewhere.

Even then, though, property is not the only thing wars are waged for. There are more than economic reasons for this one, obviously. The Germans are fighting because Hitler and some lunatics like him thought the French and English were persecuting them—and also because they had an idea they could beat the English and French and beat them badly, and thoroughly insult them afterwards too.

The war is going on because the Germans were once scared and depressed and confused and full of hatred. Economic motives increased all these unpleasant emotions, but were not their only motives. Nevertheless, as long as the world is interested in nothing more than the exploitation of economic forces, all we are going to get is one terrific war after another until there aren't any but the most primitive economic resources left to exploit!

When the Germans say they are fighting for goods, and raw materials and for "Lebensraum" and colonies, none of these are the real reasons for their going to war with such enthusiasm, because, as a matter of fact, in the same breath they claim to be idealists, and say that only the dirty capitalist democracies would fight for such base things as money, goods, raw materials, etc.

I am not sure even the Germans themselves know why they are fighting. But children do not bully one another for economic reasons, and the Nazis and Fascists long ago announced they loved killing simply for its own sake!

¶ I am in no mood to read *The Magic Mountain,* which is the kind of book I find tedious anyway. I am only willing to be excited by its metaphysical symbolism and analogies if the elementary level of the book, the surface of meaning, is also interesting. But when the surface is as tedious as this, I don't feel much like going below it.

The book is full of characters that use expressions like "Sapristi" and "Sapperlot." You find sentences like, "Doesn't your monism rather bore you?" and "What about quietism, a religion that numbers Fenelon among its disciples?" Then, with their mouths full of "chocolate-filled layer cake," they ask one another "fondly":

"Is time a function of space, or space of time? Or are they identical? Echo answers."

When echo answers, I lose interest. Metaphysics isn't any fun if it is all *sapristi* and very heavy clichés and very slow, self-satisfied speeches, and elaborate German witticisms as light as bricks.

I will admit that the book is more interesting than the Princeton Senior Poll of student opinion about the universe. But not much more.

However, I like the point about the air on the mountain, or as much as I stopped to get of the point. The mountain air is good for tuberculosis: that is, it stimulates the disease, and forces it to declare itself, and after a certain point, checks it and helps it. So Hans Castorp, who thinks he is well, is seduced by the Circes of philosophy in this Berghof to stay around until the disease also declares itself in him. Well, that is good. And I suppose there are a lot of other analogies in the book that are interesting in the same way. The application of this to the world outside is, of course, obvious.

I am also willing to admit that all these people exist, since Settembrini obviously designed the Italian Pavilion at the World's Fair. But just because they exist doesn't mean that Mann has written about them very interestingly, or not to me. Anything that exists can be written about: but the mere fact that it exists isn't enough to make the subject of a book interesting.

The mixture of materialism, disease, disinfectants; the atmosphere of inner corruption and outward spotlessness; all that fascination for nightmare romanticism, pommaded moustaches, the tomb and military honor and afternoon coffee; all those exercises, *Geheimrats,* stiff collars, heavy meals, Sanskrit verses, moustached Russian women, amateurs of optics, botany and gooseliver; all these things would make a very interesting combination to anybody who was less complacent about them than Mann, who really doesn't see anything more dangerous in all that than Sinclair Lewis saw in Babbitt.

All the material in the book is important. That damp tubercular mountain, with its microcosm on top of it, faces the flat plains of Germany and Latvia and Poland and Russia, the places where the barbarian invasions have always come from, and that is what the book is all about. A record of the barbarian invasion up to the time of the last war, or whenever it was.

Yet it is tedious.

¶ Instead of having faith, which is a virtue, and therefore nourishes the soul and gives it a healthy life,
people merely have a lot of opinions, which excite the
soul but don't give it anything to feed it, just wear
it out until it falls over from exhaustion.

An opinion isn't one thing or the other: it is neither
science nor faith, but has a little bit of either one. It is
a rationalisation bolstered up by some orthodoxy
which you happen to respect, which, naturally, starves
the mind instead of feeding it (and that is what people
who have no faith imagine faith does, but they don't
know what they are talking about, because faith is
a virtue, an active habit which cannot even pretend
to rationalise anything: it seeks what is beyond reason).

In this situation, where there are hundreds of people with no real faith, who don't really believe anything much, long inquiries are constantly being

carried out as to what various persons "believe."
Scientists, advertising men, sociologists, soldiers, crit-
ics, are all asked what they believe inasmuch as they
are scientists, advertising men, etc. Apparently there is
a separate belief appropriate to every walk of life.
Anyway, they all answer with brisk one thousand word
articles stating some opinion or other that they have
picked up somewhere. The result is enough to make
you break down and sob.

H. G. Wells has tried to spend his whole life telling
people "What he believes," that is, trying to get them
to accept his own confused opinions about the purpose of human life, if any. Since, from what I hear,
he isn't even a particularly good scientist, he hasn't
even got the basis he thinks he has for all his other
statements; but even if he were a good scientist, his
science isn't a sufficient basis for the metaphysical
and moral statements he tries to make. At the same
time he complicates his position very curiously by
denying that metaphysics or morals are really relevant
at all. His life work would be a spectacular failure if
there could be anything spectacular about someone
so completely unimportant as H. G. Wells.

It should be the great pride and strength of every
Catholic that there is no ready, ten-minute, brisk,
chatty answer to the question what we believe, except

in the words of the Apostles' Creed, which are not comprehensible to scientists anyway. It should be our greatest strength that we don't have, on the end of our tongues, a brief and pithy rationalisation for the structure and purpose of the whole universe, only a statement that, to some scientists, is a scandal: an article of faith. God created the world and everything in it for Himself, and the heavens proclaim His glory. It should be our greatest strength that we don't have any rationalisation to explain the war 'scientifically' and have no 'scientific' solution to all our economic problems.

The greatest weakness of Marxists, for example, is the readiness with which they can explain absolutely anything in brisk and chatty and pseudo-scientific terms. They have not yet begun to feel ridiculous at the way their explanations have taken to contradicting themselves completely from one day to the next: They still believe that they are being "scientific." Surely, the faith that science can contradict itself and still be science is a faith that doesn't honor science at all, because the only value science pretends to have is that it is certain and cannot cancel itself out.

Faith, on the other hand, seems to be contradicting itself, because everything we say about God is so inadequate that it always runs us head first into a paradox.

In certain things, it is even more the glory of the Catholic than of the sceptic to say "I don't know."

As a matter of fact, the true sceptic doubts in order that he may know. If there is no other certainty, he doubts so as to reduce everything to the level of his own, human, and fallible notions of certainty. But a Christian believes in order to submit all the products of his own fallible judgment to the test of a revelation that is infallible and divine and eternal—as obscure as it is infallible, obscure and mysterious because it is as simple as it is divine.

¶ All the papers tell how some cloistered nuns in New York are praying continually for peace in a novena beginning last Sunday, and, of course all Catholics should be praying every minute for peace. I hope we are. It is astounding how little we really pray, we who are supposed to believe that God hears and answers our petitions. If a person prays an hour a day, it seems tremendous: he begins to think himself a monster of asceticism.

It is a miracle, with so few people praying on this earth, that the world has any virtues at all! It is a miracle that the Battles of Flanders and France, instead of lasting a month or so, are not going on and on until every last man is wiped out. It is astonishing that, being the way we are, there should be any peace at all, on earth. But the answer is not in our wills, in our souls: it is in the weakness of our bodies.

Our bodies collapse, now, even in anticipation of battles. Armies are full of young men going mad, even before they are blown to bits, or merely shell-shocked. This is the only reason why they don't go right on fighting until they wipe out everything: their nerves break down first, they collapse from exhaustion, and have to pause, from time to time, and recover.

Nobody wonders that those people never pray who don't believe in anything, and lead their lives according to some obscure and arbitrary system of instincts and superstitions and rationalisations and prejudices and animal desires and social inhibitions. But religious people who are supposed to believe in the efficacy of prayer, and yet lead their lives by those same pagan standards, and hardly ever pray at all, are the ones that ought to be terrified, because they will be held responsible for what is happening, too! They are a stumbling block to the others, who only see in them rather cruder and poorer and less intelligent and more plebeian versions of themselves!

We have no peace because we have done nothing to keep peace, not even prayed for it! We have not even *desired* peace except for the wrong reasons: because we didn't want to get hurt, we didn't want to suffer. But if the best reason we have for desiring peace is only that we are cowards, then we are lost from the start, because the enemy only sees in our cowardice his first and most effective weapon.

If we are ever going to have peace again, we will have to hate war for some better reason than that we fear to lose our houses, our refrigerators, our cars, our legs, our lives. If we are ever to get peace, we have got to desire something more than reefers and anesthetics. That is all we seem to want: anything to avoid pain.

It is terrifying that the world doesn't wake up to this irony: that at a time when all our desire is nothing but to enjoy pleasant sensations and avoid painful sensations, there should be almost more pain, and suffering and brutality and horror, and more *helplessness* to do anything about it than there ever was before!

¶ What (besides making lists of the vices of our age) are some of the greatest vices of our age?

To begin with, people began to get self-conscious about the fact that their misconducted lives were going to pieces: so, instead of ceasing to do the things that made them ashamed and unhappy, they made it a new rule that they must never be ashamed of the things they did. There was to be only one capital sin: to be ashamed. That was how they thought they could solve the problem of sin, by abolishing the term.

Another vice of the last hundred and fifty years has grown out of all the facile rationalisations of cyclical movements in history, leading to the belief that with every new year we were witnessing the return of some pattern of events that had already taken shape once before in history. Now that we have got back to the rebirth of Druidism, the fall of Rome, the new Golden Age, and the plagues of Egypt, the whole thing is too complicated for anything but total destruction.

We are developing a new superstition: that people who think too much about a certain disease will give it to themselves by suggestion; we get ulcers from worrying about them. If we don't worry about them, says the converse of this argument, we won't get any diseases.

We have another superstition, like this one. If we all agree that war is unpleasant, and that we don't want it, then we won't have to fight. We think that just because we don't want to fight, nobody will ever come and take away our ice cream sodas, incidentally killing us. This is bound to happen if, in the same breath, we accuse them of being dirty dogs for coveting our ice cream sodas.

Then of course we have the vice of thinking that because something is successful, it is therefore valuable: the worth of a thing is in its profit to us.

Also we love facts for their own sake, in contradiction to the superstition I just mentioned. The radio is full of question bees and information programs, and everybody reads digest magazines which list as many facts as can be crammed into the smallest possible space. At the same time, the very hardest thing in the world to get is any real news about the war. We know the bare fact that France has been beaten. But what

is going on there? It might as well be some country
in the moon.

It is hard to conceive France as a nation which has
now been crowded into its most humble provinces:
the Auvergne, the Dauphiné, the Limousin, etc. What
will be the first public utterance of the government
once the nation has collected itself together in its
diminished and dishonoured state? How will they
express themselves, ever? What will be the first book
printed in the new, captive France? What will be the
first exhibition of paintings? All this is hard to imagine, particularly if the capital is going to be some
place like Clermont-Ferrand.

August 21, 1940
OLEAN, NEW YORK

¶ Maybe today was the day when I should have asked myself what has happened to the summer. But it was in many respects a good day, colder and very clear. Tonight when I was walking on the road in the woods, I saw the moon was well past full, and moonlight looked colder than I had ever seen it before. Streaks of mist, like bacon, hung over the valley.

Back in the cabin Ed Rice had been reading, in a pamphlet that had once belonged with an album of tangos, that many people had broken their legs doing the tango.

¶ This was the first time I ever went to Yorkville: to
see the film of the war in Poland, a year ago. The
Germans took a lot of trouble to get those pictures,
and the propaganda, of course, was not in the pictures
but in the cutting and the commentary. (The same
pictures were used all over again against the Germans,
later, by the March of Time.)

It showed no dead men, nobody getting killed,
nobody even getting roughed up. A couple of Poles,
in a great crowd of prisoners, appeared with bandages
on. They showed one dead horse, with a great swollen
belly. Otherwise, no death.

On the other hand there were hundreds of feet, it
seemed, of destroyed material and houses. All this
destruction was completely dehumanized. You saw a
lot of razed buildings, blasted bridges, wrecked trains,
piles of captured guns and other nondescript stuff. It
was like watching hours of filming of a great garbage

dump, and the whole thing soon got very nauseating and stupid. After that, when they did show men, even the men looked dehumanized, and appeared to be nothing but more equipment.

The Germans looked like good equipment, the Poles looked like cheap equipment, slightly spoiled. Otherwise they were the same. It almost seemed to be the point of the picture that these men had ceased to be people, and were nothing but very good equipment, sound, reliable and tireless German equipment, manufactured by the Fuehrer.

But there was one shot of some Germans riding by on caissons, dead tired, and some of them slumbering. Suddenly one man got in the eye of the camera, and gave back the straightest and fiercest and most resentful look I ever saw. Great rings surrounded his eyes which were full of exhaustion, pain and protest. And he kept staring, turning his head and fixing his eyes on the camera as he went by demanding to be seen as a person, and not as the rest of the cattle. The censors should have cut him out, because he succeeded. You began to realise how tired and disgusted all those soldiers must have been. It added great weight to the effect of all the garbage that had gone before. What a thing to be proud of! To have turned one whole country into a junk heap!

There was nothing insidious or subtle about the commentary, which was in English. It was dogmatic and blatant and clumsy, and wouldn't have fooled anybody except a German.

The general effect of the film was not terror, or anything at all dramatic: you just got oppressed by the drabness of a lot of tired soldiers and a lot of rubble and garbage.

The shots of Hitler himself were just as drab and dull as all the rest. He looks like nothing: an insignificant little guy with a pointed nose and a dejected mouth, down at the corners, like a tired washwoman's.

Once in a while there would be a surprising picture: the sky above burning Warsaw (lying low on the horizon) was filled not with black smoke but huge white clouds, hanging still and piling up like thunderheads and filling that whole quarter of the compass. There was a telephoto shot of Gdynia under fire which was interesting because of the crazy telephoto perspective, but not much more. There is evidently nothing beautiful or exciting to be found in war at all, because these photographers must have tried their best. It was simply ugly, all the way through.

The really ugly parts were about the bombers. You didn't see anything repulsive happen, or terrible or frightening: but the bombers themselves looked like big, malevolent, outlandish bugs.

The most actively obscene shot in the whole picture was one of a bomber releasing a stick of bombs which fell away from under its belly in a group: it was like some vile beetle laying eggs in the air, or dropping its filth.

There was nothing about the picture from beginning to end that wasn't squalid. I don't know what I expected: perhaps I thought the war had some new horror to it that I hadn't imagined. If it has, that never got shown, and isn't likely to be, either. This is a picture supposed to favor war, and show how much was accomplished by a war. The pictures were evidently truer than they were meant to be. It is no joke that the world is going to turn into something infinitely repulsive and horrible when it is remade in the image of people who believe in this kind of thing: and the tragedy of that is, if we fight Hitler, we will become like him, too, we will turn into something just as dirty as he is. If we are going to beat him, we will have to.

Everybody in Yorkville looked very peaceable except the waiters standing in the doors of the restaurants and bars.

❡ Sunday and yesterday there were great earthquakes in Rumania and great windstorms in America: that is a neat combination for Nostradamus to put into one of his illiterate quatrains. Now tomorrow Greece will probably cave in, precipitating the Italian army into the sea, or London will be finally wiped out, or Hitler will fall downstairs and break his hip.

I have an idea Hitler will die of nothing spectacular, like a bomb, but will succumb to some children's disease, like the chicken pox or the mumps.

It is a very violent and dangerous world, even around here, I saw a shooting star. One of my students was beating up a freshman when he fell into a hedge and got a thorn so deep in his hand the doctor had to cut it out. Father C. is mad at *The New Yorker* for being anti-Catholic and I am mad at it for being anti-funny. Gibney has got a cold and Lax is afraid to drive Gibney's car, so I don't see anybody. The football coach has been bitten by Father H.'s black spaniel. The football team has lost another game. Somebody told me that a pig, when it attacks a human being, gores out the entrails and eats them but will touch positively nothing else. I saw what I thought was a photograph of the Three Ritz Brothers dressed up as women, but it turned out to be the Three Andrews Sisters in their ordinary clothes. Somebody told me that the College's Junior Prom could not be held in Bradford because nobody could drive the short distance back, after it, without running into a tree. They tried once and that was the result. This is a very violent and dangerous world.

¶ Kierkegaard, describing the metaphysics of the "Dark Night of the Soul" or the bottom of the abyss of faith as only a few men ever possessed it, speaks of Abraham's trial, when he was commanded to sacrifice Isaac, as an example of the incomprehensible tribulations of this "dark Night."

Abraham was put in a situation that was beyond duty, beyond mere obedience to God, in any intelligible sense. It was a trial nobody could understand, not even Abraham himself. The situation is so incomprehensible, that any attempt by Abraham to explain himself to Isaac, for instance, would be ruinous, and any attempt to explain it to himself, even, might prove to be a disaster.

Kierkegaard distinguishes what he calls "infinite renunciation" in a hero who dies for some exalted, but recognisable duty, and becomes a teacher by example,

133

sacrificing himself for the sake of a universal value
that everyone can understand, as for example a mar-
tyr dying for his faith; he distinguishes this renunciation of the "hero" from the incomprehensible renunciation of the perfect saint, I forget Kierkegaard's
word for him, whose renunciation can only be valuable in the sight of God since to men it is meaningless,
or even absurd. God's command to Abraham to sacrifice Isaac has nothing to do with ethics, the ordinary
standards of which it violates. To treat the situation
as an ethical problem (can a man commit a murder
if God commands it?) leads to nothing but a series of
horrible contradictions and futilities. This whole
problem doesn't even arise: because, to begin with,
God is unlike any other person, in His commands,
since He knows their outcome before he gives them.
He is not commanding Isaac's murder, because Isaac
is already saved, and the real Lamb of God already
seen as sacrificed instead. There is no question of
murder, or of anything that has a positive or negative
value that can be judged by ethics here. Kierkegaard
calls this a case of "teleological suspension of ethics,"
and the reason for this suspension is that in this problem, which involves Abraham's being tested, through
dread, in the immediate presence of God, no other
relationships, no ethical relationships intervene.

Isaac's life is not really at stake, Isaac doesn't enter into the real drama at all.

It would be an ethical problem though (says Kierkegaard), if Abraham thought he was going to kill Isaac. But here is another complexity: Abraham, carrying out, in obedience to God, all the preparations for sacrifice, at the same time believes that God's goodness is such that at the last moment the sacrifice will be unnecessary, Isaac will be saved.

He has absolutely no way of imagining how this is going to be made possible, for, on the contrary, he has God's absolute command to kill Isaac, and this command is so absolute he must not even stop and think for two seconds, debate about it at all, try to explain anything to Isaac or to Sara or even to himself. Yet up to the last minute, when he raises the sword over his son, he has to believe, absolutely against all hope, that God will save Isaac. And then Isaac is, as a matter of fact, saved.

Kierkegaard may or may not be writing a drama of his own, which may or may not have something to do with the Abraham of the Old Testament. But the important thing is that the terrible and anguishing paradox of the dark night of absolute faith in God is certainly made as clear here as anybody has made it since St. John of the Cross.

All paradoxes are comprehensible, except perhaps the paradoxes that face a few rare souls, who are taken apart by God and confronted not with a test that can be decided in ethical terms, but a test that is according to the ways of God, the ways of eternity, in which nothing is fully comprehensible to us, and nothing is known except terror and silence, and a command.

And this command, since it commands us to do God's will, commands us to do something we believe to be good, but, according to any standards we are able to understand, the command is either fantastic or, in the case of Abraham, seemingly evil.

Kiekegaard applies this notion to the Sacrifice commanded to Abraham. It can also be used to make understandable the dread with which Our Blessed Mother must have received the message of the angel, and the great depth of the humility of her consent, which is, again, far beyond any obedience we can comprehend, and also involves a "teleological suspension of ethics" (the mockery of blasphemers is one of the consequences of this suspension).

"Be it done unto me according to Thy word!" is infinitely beyond mere heroism. Mary took upon herself, with these words, a responsibility utterly unintelligible in human terms. These words are all that

can be said: "Be it done according to Thy Word."
Further comment is impossible.

So, those who have had to suffer, in this way, before
God, says Kierkegaard, rising higher than heroes do
not become greater than heroes in the eyes of the
world, but can only become as nonentities in the eyes
of the world, because we cannot understand.

Nobody ever realised the great sanctity of the
Immaculate Mother of God, because she was so far
above what could be known as heroism that she
merely seemed a completely ordinary, poor woman.
Kierkegaard concludes, from this notion of the essential incommunicability of the highest form of religious experience, that those who possess it are in no
way remarkable on account of it, outwardly, and are,
in fact, undistinguishable from everybody else, while
the lesser hero, whose heroism only reaches the limit
of the highest, ethical sacrifice, is immediately remarkable to all in his lifetime, and dazzles everybody by
his heroic virtue.

The two states, I think, can be illustrated in the life
of St. Francis. Before the stigmatisation, on Mount
Alverno, he was the saint that preached to the birds,
played the fiddle on two sticks, sang to the Lord in
French, and was an absolute hero of childlike poverty

and humility and love. But by a "teleological suspension of ethics," another "tragedy" like that of Gethsemani and Calvary was visited upon him, and he shared the stigmata, that is, the shame of the most terrible insult that was ever perpetrated: the wounds made in the hands, feet and side of God by His own creatures.

At once, in the story, he ceases to be a dramatic figure altogether. Carrying in the world the marks of Christ's apparent defeat and of his own apparent defeat (in the government of his own order), there is nothing dramatic even about these, because he is now beyond drama, and beyond romance. He is a strange, colorless, hunched up little man, riding, speechless, with his hands bound up in rags and concealed under his sleeves!

¶ Chaucer, in his introduction to Sir Thopas, describes himself as if he were Stephen Dedalus. Maybe all Aristotelians have a tendency to turn into James Joyce.

I thought of buying Dylan Thomas' *Portrait of the Artist as a Young Dog* but refrained, believing the title would be the only thing good about it.

I learned how to read Blake's "To the Muses" which I have been reading all these years without comprehension. I read it to my sympathetic evening class. They shook their heads. I explained "the green corners of the earth." They fainted, maybe. I think they were shocked, that, in another connection, the sun should come forth as a bridegroom from the chamber, rejoicing as a giant to run his course.

Last night I tore a handful of pages out of last year's Journal. It is nice to have a Journal, written at great length one year, to fall upon, when you are idle, the next. You sit like a king and read a few pages and then reach out and tear them from the book and throw them away: you have read the day's news.

The reason is God's delegate to sit in judgment upon itself, says St. Bernard.

Today was another of my days for believing Wordsworth to be a madman. Only his later poems, I mean mostly sonnets, can persuade me he wasn't a crazy phony. Today I read "Lines left on a seat under a yew tree." What confusion!

Outside, in the snow, I heard a rifle shot under the pine trees beyond the greenhouses. Once they had a pen of hounds out there, that nobody knew what to do with. They all descended from one or two strays that turned up and had since multiplied, fed by the friars.

I think of the Hieronymus Bosch "Adoration of the Kings" in the Metropolitan. People who don't like art will tolerate the surrealism of Bosch on the ground that he lived in the old days and therefore didn't know any better. What an insult, that this degenerate and very barbarous age should imagine that any artist, let alone one who could draw as true a Christ-child as Bosch, could paint half-consciously, and not mean what he said, as if this clumsy and stupid age was the only one that ever knew what it was doing! As a matter of fact, I wonder if there ever was an age in which people knew *less* clearly what they were doing!

I opened a grammar book, and came upon a sentence to be analysed. It read: "Mr. Edison's motto is *'If you hustle while you wait you will succeed.'* " I have scarcely been so happy over anything since all that stuff about Victor Hugo in Cocteau's *Grand Ecart*. "If you hustle while you wait . . ." Come with me and let us worship the superhuman wisdom of the immortal Edison, whose wire trinkets are being holed away for the war in a shelter able to resist the heaviest bombs, which is a lot more than you or I will ever see, Charles!

"Hustle while you wait!"

If you are forced to stand in one place for a few minutes, at least do not stand still. Turn somersaults, cartwheels, handsprings. Get in everybody's way. Be a success.

While waiting for that big appointment, ceaselessly climb up and down and all over the furniture of the outer office. Terrify the help. Make yourself known. They will never forget you.

When you sit down to dinner, do not waste the precious moments that elapse while the maid is serving up the food. Practise whisking the cloth off the table without disturbing any of the plates. Bet you can't! Try!

Waiting for the subway? Do not stand in one place! Knock somebody down, start a fight! You will make a real impression! So hustle, Charlie, hustle while you wait and in the end they will keep your false teeth in a bombproof shelter, far from the cities where will be heard the sirens of the ambulances carrying the little children to the hospitals rigged up in tents among the ruins of the buildings.

Vestimentum tuum candidum quasi nix, et facies tua sicut sol.

❡ This feast is especially important not only because it is a feast of the Mother of God, but because it is a modern feast, and because nothing is done by chance, it must be singularly significant that this Feast was instituted for *us*.

This feast of the purest created person, of all that God made the most perfect and the most excellent creature, most excellent in wisdom and power and beauty and love, of whom it is said *"Tota pulchra es, Maria, et macula originalis non est in te."* Yet the doctrine of this Immaculate Conception, emphasizing beyond anything that had ever been said before the terrific purity and love of the Blessed Virgin, and celebrating the most perfect of all created beauty, became dogma in a century which more than any other was absorbed in its own abominable ugliness.

Her Immaculate Conception became dogma in a time when everybody was plunging head over heels into materialism and sensual vulgarity.

Now that all this blasphemous ugliness and greed have borne fruit in the worst war in history, we must try to turn with a deep reverence of devotion to the Immaculate Mother of God.

It is blasphemous for us to treat this feast as if it were the feast of some callow little girl who was merely ignorant of sin, or the feast of some nice, pensive lady in a white gown who lacked either imagination or passion. This is the Feast of the most perfect love of God, which love was more powerful than the Archangels, because it was this immaculate love that crushed the serpent of selfishness and hatred. The purity and glory of the Immaculate Conception defy all imagination.

Purity in the Christian sense is not merely a negation—the absence of carnal indulgence. It is something positive, constructive, and fruitful: it is the perfection of a love that contains within itself the capacity for the highest fruitfulness, spiritual fruitfulness, and the purity of Our Lady was a love pure enough to become an unfailing source of life for "all the living."

Through Mary's love, through the purity of her faith, God has given to us the Word of Life: and the Word made flesh, with the consent of her pure love has dwelt among us, full of grace and truth.

¶ I will not soon forget how happy I was to get back here from New York. Not that there was anything wrong with New York: but it was delightful to come into my room here and see the pictures tacked on the door, and the bed made up with clean sheets.

In New York—no movies, no plays, no circuses, no hockey games, no "Heaven on Ice" or whatever they called the thing. No anything but work and the Columbia library, and seeing Lax and Gibney off to Virginia. And, last of all, yesterday, three eggnogs out at Northport among those giggling Jane Austen girls: pretty, flaxhaired, having visited Sweden, having studied music.

They giggled and flirted with Rice. They wanted to ask their ouija board if Rice was in love.

Their mother swore she liked the ruined churches at Visby and wanted to put more Seagram's into the

eggnogs. They offered, to each and all, marzipan on a
plate.

One had a record from *The Marriage of Figaro* for
Christmas.

Foolishly I talked of Bloy's book *Celle qui Pleure*
and the old lady thought, concerning the apparitions
of the Virgin at La Salette: "Someone might have
imposed on those children," meaning someone did.

I spoke to her about it. On either side, just out of
range of direct vision, her two daughters sat and
listened, out of focus.

It got dull when everybody started talking about
Roosevelt.

Gerdy was or was not peeved when everybody refused to leave at 9:30 (his suggestion) just after we had
got there. Gerdy fidgeted a lot. One of the girls was his
girl.

They were tall girls, their flax hair was uncut and
hung in hanks down their backs. They wore velvet
dresses. They smiled continually and had me figured
for a priest, at which I scarcely know whether to be
delighted or annoyed. To be a priest is in my eyes a
good thing, but in the eyes of two little dames wanting
to play around, a bad thing.

And so this is the New Year, 1941. I tried to tell

myself: a year of terrors, but the sun was out. It may well be, just the same. I am the worst of all prophets: prophecy is the one thing, besides mathematics and being a soldier, that I am certain I have no gift for. Being an ice-man I am not certain about, never having tried.

¶ "Formerly mankind did not have such a need (for suffering). Things would be better if men would praise God more. Even a little flower can give us occasion to thank God and to praise Him. The savior permits suffering, to punish certain sins, to test the fidelity of those who love Him, and to give men an opportunity to help others. The sufferings are never so great that a person cannot bear them, *or must be unhappy,* if he has the Savior with him."

—THERESA NEUMANN.

¶ I renounce, with the greatest alacrity in the world, the following literary projects:

1) Writing a story about a man who owns a dog named Caesar. Somewhere in the course of the story someone would come in with a pail of old bones, garbage, pieces of gristle, chicken guts, melon rinds, etc., and would say: "What am I supposed to do with these old bones, garbage, pieces of gristle, etc?" At which the owner of the dog would wittily reply: "Render unto Caesar the things that are Caesar's."

2) Writing a story about a bantamweight prize-fighter named "Kid Promiscuous."

3) Writing a story about four people, two old, two young, all of them models, who had never seen each other before, and who had to pose together for a color photo advertising some product or other, as if they were a family: Father, mother, daughter, grandson.

4) I have never renounced, because never yet

thought of, the idea of writing a story about some people in an air-raid shelter during an air-raid. Now I have thought of the idea and now I renounce it.

5) The story about the revolution in a Caribbean island, which was to have been a *Collier's* story, was renounced in June 1939 and stays renounced. The island was called San Jaime. I renounce the *Collier's* story, as a literary form, forever.

January 16, 1941

¶ Bloy's *The Woman Who Was Poor* is some novel.

There are two parts, with a great difference between them, and the second is immeasurably better than the first. It contains a love story that is perhaps the best love story I ever read. It ends up with a mystical vision, led up to by a series of scenes as simple and clean as pictures by Blake (I don't mean illustrations to the Prophetic Books!).

The beginning, on the other hand, is muddled and disconcerting until you look at it in relation to the end. I found a lot of the descriptions of artists and writers unbelievable and embarrassing. I was a little suspicious of Gacougnol, and still do not believe Marchenoir stroked the tiger in the zoo. Gacougnol's death, and the terror inspired in taxi drivers by Leopold were all right.

The death of the child in the second part is completely terrifying.

The scene at Parc la Valliere, with the two old women sitting in the windows of their house, like a punch and judy, exchanging insults intended for Leopold and his wife (a diabolical persecution) is also terrific.

I reflect that Bloy called himself a pilgrim of the Holy Sepulchre and that a critic of him, Ernest Sellière, pointing out that Bloy never actually went to the Holy Sepulchre, is highly incensed at such inconsistent madness.

I often wonder, since reading that, how Sellière avoids tripping over the big millstone he must have hanging around his neck, and falling into a river, and being drowned. But I dare say he has just enough instinctive prudence to sit on his millstone, and perhaps read the German edition of *Paris Soir,* in which he will certainly find no such madness as Bloy's at all!

¶ Quick! Quick! Let's get down the phenomenal results of the last two minutes' meditation on the art of writing. Pay your penny and pull up a broken chair and listen to the arguments of the author trying to catch himself out in right field without a glove.

Q. Don't you think that by now you are big enough to write short stories?

A. Well, that's interesting. I just have written two short stories.

Q. Ah, so! So so so! Pull yourself up straight and conceal the gap between your vest and the top of your pants and tell me how you think you feel.

A. Rotten.

Q. Rotten?

A. Yes. Never wanted to write them anyway.

Q. Why did you?

A. Sense of duty, I guess.

Q. Duty? To whom?

A. Caesar, I guess.

Q. O go on!

A. Yes, you heard me, Caesar. Render unto Caesar
the things that are easier. Let me tell you, if I were to
render these sorry documents to God, I'd be the shag-
giest of the goats upon the Day of Judgment.

Q. What's the matter? Your stories lewd, maybe?

A. No, stupid. Bad.

Q. Explain.

A. I feel like a card cheat in the Athenaeum Club in
London, getting the absent treatment from the
Prime Minister in my shabby artistic conscience.

Q. Cheating's allowed, so long as the bombs are
dropping.

A. Who said?

Q. Well, what's this about cheating?

A. I wrote two stories with plots. It was like when I
was fourteen. I wrote stories with plots then, too. And
in these stories, I didn't speak my own mind, or ana-
lyse myself one bit. The whole thing was sheer artifice.

Q. Maybe they'll sell.

A. You cheap weasel.

Q. Okay. What's wrong with artifice?

A. It's a lie, that's what.

Q. O, a platonist!

A. Don't confuse me with insults.

Q. Well, come on, what did the stories have besides a plot?

A. Characters!

Q. My, but you're sly! Tell me some more. Good characters?

A. Dolts, stupids, clods, the whole pack of them. Blocks; logs; stones; earth!

Q. That is regrettable.

A. It comes of cheating, that's what.

Q. But supposing the stories sell like hot cakes?

A. Then I'll cry like a boy with a mouthful of mustard.

Q. Why?

A. I love my poverty, I really do. Poverty is freedom, riches a curse.

Q. Couldn't you take the dough and fling it away to the poor?

A. That would be robbing Peter to pay Paul. I'm poor too. Who am I to act rich? That is the evil of money: you act rich. It isn't bad in itself. Leave the stuff lay.

Q. Aw, you're crazy.

A. Maybe I am, but I'm going to tear them two

stories up in shreds and go away and write something
that's more like Joyce, before my style goes and gets
clear and silly and precious. Good night, Harry.
Think it over, Harry. Think it over.

February 4, 1941

¶ Secretly in my heart this morning I believe my
novel is not so bad. Sure as anything that means it is
now being rejected by somebody I never even heard
of, and the splash of the rejection stirs up silent,
obscure waves that reach out blindly to me in a
soundless cry for sympathy: "Help!" cries the novel,
"I have just been rejected again!"

I do not mention which novel, it goes for both.*

This time last year *The Labyrinth* had just been
rejected by Macmillan. Since then it has been to
Viking, Knopf, Harcourt Brace, then to the agent
Curtis Brown, who sent it to Modern Age, Atlantic
Monthly Books, McBride, and now Carrick and

---

* There were at this time two novels going the rounds of the publishers in manuscript: *The Labyrinth* and the *Man in the Sycamore
Tree.*

158

Evans. Carrick and Evans' "No" has not yet reached me.

So many bad books get printed, why can't *my* bad book get printed?

Q. Well, make up your mind: is *Euphues* tedious, or isn't it?

A. Boy! Some parts of *Euphues* are the worst stuff I ever read!

Q. Ha! Ha! You've certainly changed your tune in the last few months.

A. Parts of it are still all right.

Q. So you finally found out the difference between *Euphues* and Castiglione's *Courtier!*

A. So what?

Q. Castiglione's *Courtier* is a real book, and *Euphues* isn't.

A. You're Q. You should be asking questions, not making statements. But now I'll ask one: where's my copy of the *Courtier?* What thief has it?

Q. How do you know you didn't give it away according to your well known plans of last year, hey?

A. You said it. How do I know?

Q. Incidentally, now that we have mentioned the plan you once entertained this time last year, of entering a monastery: how does it look now?

A. The same. But I think I'd be a Trappist.

Q. Now you're joking!

A. You think so?

¶ The poems of Dylan Thomas look valuable even
typographically, the way they stand out on the page.

His writing depends on a terrific coherence of sound
and imagery overlying an incoherence, or maybe even
lack of ideas. His poems are, then, kind of abstractions,
but abstractions full of tremendous, sinewy craft and
wit and inventiveness and vividness.

There is nothing tinny or chatty about him.

Thomas has a couple of tricks that could be overdone by someone less smart than he: one of them is
shuffling around the functions of the five senses so as
to pair them off unnaturally: the eye hears, the ear
feels, the lip sees.

He writes mostly about hell, and like most of the
living poets he has set himself a task: to walk through
hell describing everything as if there were no good
and evil, and only avoiding one thing: the refusal to

see the objects of his experience. All the while there is one other problem: remaining sane.

Virgil pointed out all the damned to Dante, but covered the traveller's eyes for fear he should see the head of Medusa and turn to stone. Dylan Thomas and the others of this generation want to go through hell without Virgil, and hope they will not be turned to stone by Medusa. But they won't say they won't look, even at that terrifying spectacle.

His prose style is something like Robert Green or Thomas Dekker in the rogue and plague pamphlets of the sixteenth century, but I can't read it for horrors. He gets some very striking effects by describing living organisms as if they were things crudely put together out of wood and string and nondescript materials. His syntax is very solid.

I thought that perhaps reading the titles of his poems (all first lines) down the page of the table of contents would be like a parody of one of his poems: but that wasn't so at all, which is, maybe, a sign of strength.

I pick out of the book some images I liked:

The fences of the light are down
All but the briskest riders thrown,
And worlds hang on the trees.

or

The force that through the green fuse drives the flower
Drives my green age; that blasts the roots of trees
Is my destroyer.

He is interested in Eucharistic images, not always the best way. This is okay:

Once in this bread
The oat was merry in the wind.
Man broke the sun, pulled the wind down . . .

The hand that signed the treaty bred a fever. . . .

Now Jack my fathers let the time-faced crook,
Death flashing from his sleeve,
With swag of bubbles in a seedy sack,
Sneak down the stallion grave.

Everything he writes is striking and easy to remember. I feel awed to think there is this good poet, and only a year older than I am. I used to be awed that Joe Louis, heavyweight champion of the world, was almost as young as I!

¶ If I pray for peace, that prayer is only justified if it means one thing: not that the war may end, the fighting stop, and murdering and injustice continue some other way. To pray merely for the war to stop, and some fake armistice to be signed is not to pray for peace.

If I pray for peace, abstractly speaking it makes sense if I pray for a "just peace," although I do not know what, in political terms, would constitute a just peace now, and I am totally unable to get any relevance, politically, out of the term.

But when I pray for peace I pray for the following miracle. That God move all men to pray and do penance and recognize each one his own great guilt, because we are all guilty of this war, in a way. Bloy says somewhere, of a murderer, that all the people were a tree of which this murderer was only one of the fruits, and that applies to Hitler: we are a tree, of which he is one of the fruits, and we all nourish him, and he thrives most of all on our hatred and condemnation of him, when that condemnation disregards our own guilt, and piles the responsibility for everything upon somebody else's sins!

When I pray for peace, I pray for this miracle. That the whole world begin to lament and fast, that when all the guilty have done penance, the terrible punishment which is now falling upon everybody may at least be lifted from the backs of the comparatively innocent!

But the whole world is going clean contrary to this. The ones that hate war, hate it because of its sufferings, not because it is unjust, and those who have ideas of justice are all too busy seeking their own advantage rather than that of mankind as a whole: they *want* war.

¶ First it was bright, then there was an interesting storm, with snow flying parallel to the ground, then it got bright again with a Rome-Florida-Bermuda sky making a holiday over the very white hills. Small orange clouds, dazzling with a light and rich and lovely internal fire hung still and very high in the clean atmosphere like clouds in a Giovanni Bellini picture, and the whole thing was a lot gayer than any carnival I ever dreamed of or heard of.

Walking home from town I saw a crazy collie racing around and around a house like a streak, herding it like a herd of sheep. His barks rang down the sunny road, and disappeared. He was also afraid of the cars: when he was still, a passing car would set him running again, streaking around the house.

God made this one very swell day. Past the place where the dog was, I reached the line of trees where

the road goes over the rise and you see the college
and monastery off across the fields. There the sun was
bright on a white house right beside the road, with a
bright green roof and a bright red chimney: never
saw such sharp colors, or such clean light in the cold
air.

On the way up, past this place, in the storm, I now
remembered, all the houses over on that side of the
road had been on their knees in the snow, praying
like fat old women to be saved from the terrors of this
thick and fast-flying snow.

¶ I was the first one at the Draft Board for the medical,
and got out about a quarter to nine, or nine o'clock,
into the icy wind and snow. It was cold standing
around in your skin passing from doctor to doctor.
The room was full of tongue-tied doctors and tongue-
tied, naked farmboys, nobody even trying to express
anything much. One stands on a metal scale. Another
holds his hand over one eye and squints at a big chart
beginning with an O.

They didn't do much to me except take the blood
out of my arm for the Wasserman test. The blood
looked surprisingly dark in the test tube. Then they
corked it and left it to cook in a big simmering basin
over a gas ring. All this, for no rational cause, made
me full of almost unbearable, but silent feelings of
protest.

Shortly after that they made a big to-do over my

teeth, and all came and looked at my mouth in a
bunch, and the doctor told me I would probably be in
1-B, and I didn't really believe him.

Nothing much else was done to me, except some
very cursory, but humiliating investigations. As an
afterthought they knocked me on the knee for my re-
flex.

Then I put on my clothes, and one of the doctors,
with an apologetic sort of a smirk, gave me a little
folder with a picture of some soldiers leaning out of
a train, waving. *"So long, boys!"* said the folder,
"Take care of yourselves!" which, if it was meant to be
consoling, didn't console me. I had already dismissed
from my mind as impossible the idea that I would be
in 1-B.

Inside the folder was a whole lot of advice about
venereal disease, and (for those who still were unim-
pressed) hints on contraception.

Q. Well then, how are you going to begin?

A. Chronologically, perhaps: The *Felsenbrau* sign
that impressed me as we came in to the city on the
Big Four train. It was up on a big real Fels-cliff. Light
went on and off. *Felsenbrau—aged in the hills. Fels-*
enbrau—aged in the hills. My only question was, did
Felsenbrau themselves go and hack up that monad-
nock of a cliff where the sign was?

Q. You are full of ideas about Cincinnati, since
you express yourself so volubly even on so small a
matter as this. What other thoughts do you have concerning the city?

A. How many "n"s in its name?

Q. Have you expressed this thought elsewhere?

A. Yes, on a postcard to Lax.

Q. Did you put in that postcard everything you at
first intended?

A. No. I omitted the statement that the Cincinnati

R.R. Station was as big and as pretty as the whole N.Y. World's Fair of 1939.

Q. Why did you leave this out? Taste?

A. No. Forgot.

Q. You had thought it up before? In the station itself?

A. Yace!

Q. What other thoughts did you have in the Cincinnati station?

A. Whether to go on at once to Louisville.

Q. Obviously enough, you did not, since here you sit on the 3rd floor of the quiet Hotel Parkview, overlooking the statue of General Garfield (president of U.S.). I take it you were attracted by the city?

A. O, I intended to stop over anyway. But I was instantly seduced by its freshness, as they say.

Q. Who say?

A. They. Them. Rousseau. Voltaire.

Q. Over there? Was Europe a success?

A. I thought of that in the coffee shop of the Hotel Simpson, Stinton or Stimson. I thought of that title. Of J.W. Krutch speaking the title (his own words) and Mark Van Doren laughing at J.W. Krutch saying with a sniff, "Was Europe a Success?" Then I thought of me laughing at something said by Seymour. Previously, in the train, near Springfield, Ohio, I had thought of Seymour's name for the hero of his novel—

Simon Kelwey and wondered if he lived anywhere
but Long Beach, would he have made it Calloway?
Kelwey—a very Jewish non-Jewish name! The kind
a guy called Calvag would change his name to. (There
goes a fire engine.)

Q. What else occurred to you in the Hotel Stimson,
Slimpton or Shimpman?

A. That the dinner I had there was the worst food I
had ever eaten. That I had been eating grapefruit and
eggs all day (travelling), instead of potatoes and beans
and bread, as at school (fasting, working). And was
this fasting?

Q. Was it?

A. The food was no pleasure; especially the vege-
tables.

Q. What is the first thing you remember about
Galion, Ohio?

A. That I cleverly called it *The Tobacco Road of the
Universe,* to a woman, when we stood on the plat-
form of the Erie Station desolate, while hopeless of
ever seeing any taxis to take us over to the Big Four
Station.

Q. Did anything subsequently bear out your idea that
Galion was cheerless?

A. Yes: the Steel Burial Vault Works, next to the Big

Four Station. Best steel burial vaults in the world.
Worst station.

Q. What trains were late at Galion?

A. The Erie, 36 minutes. The Big 4, 20 minutes.
Normally there is a wait of one hour between trains.
If the Big 4 had been on time the wait would have
been reduced to 24 minutes. As it was, we waited 44
minutes.

Q. To whom did you converse?

A. Correction please: *with* whom. Well, the principal
of some elementary school in Youngstown.

Q. What acquaintance of yours from Youngstown,
whom she had never heard of, did you mention to
her?

A. Bob Kirk, Columbia '38, expelled for rioting.

Q. Were you surprised she had not heard of him?

A. Well, so what! Let's get back to Cincinnati!!

Q. As you wish. How did you happen to get to the
Hotel Slimpton in the first place, to eat, since you are
yourself staying at the Hotel Parkview, and writing
with their pen?

A. I was walking, looking for a place to eat.

Q. What places had you passed up?

A. Old Vienna, Mill's Rest., the B and G, The
Canary Cottage, The Netherland Plaza Julep Bar,

Wiggins' Bar—where it was very crowded and beery.

Q. O, holier than thou! Why did you pick the
Simpson?

A. Looked like a good hotel. But what did I find?
Emptiness; old ladies!

Q. Neither *crowded* nor *beery*.

A. Shut up!

Q. What public buildings, or buildings, impress you
in Cincinnati?

A. The Station. The housing project on the way from
the Station—not in itself, but as a symptom of Cincinnati's good-will in making a nice clean new avenue,
through a slum, to the station.

Q. Others?

A. The Cincinnati Club. St. Francis Xavier's Church.
The other, newer church, on 8th Street just beyond
Vine, where I hope to go to mass tomorrow morning
(Palm Sunday).

Q. What else pops into your head, concerning Cincinnati?

A. Count Cincinnati, in E. Waugh's *Vile Bodies*.

Q. Where are you glad you didn't take a room?

A. The Y.M.C.A. The Interlaken Plaza, or whatever
it is. The Slipshod.

Q. Come, no puns. Where did you first tell the taxi-
driver to go, before changing your mind?

A. The Y.M.C.A.

Q. I thought so! Well: what other project have you abandoned in Cincinnati?

A. Going on to Louisville by bus. Looking for an art musuem, it is so late. Taking any interest in Covington.

Q. What is Cincinnati full of?

A. Starlings, going north. Soldiers, going north, south, east and west and, all too soon, to Europe. Warmer air than St. Bona's. Happiness. Southerners. Old houses, distinguished, dilapidated. A pleasant air of charm; a character of its own.

Q. With whom did you converse concerning the draft?

A. The elevator boy in the Hotel. He said: "They're going to reach out and get me."

Q. What surprised you about him?

A. His age. He seemed to be 18; is, or says he is, 34.

Q. What contribution did you make to the discussion?

A. The statement that I had been deferred: unexplained, as I had a frog in my throat.

Q. What movies tempted you to come in their portals?

A. None. Lay off the portals.

Q. To what other cities do you prefer Cincinnati?

A. Buffalo, Erie, Dayton, Columbus, Cleveland, New

York, Boston, Washington, Richmond, Miami, etc.,
etc.

Q. You name almost all the cities in America you
have seen!

A. Yes, as a matter of fact, I do. Cincinnati is the best
city I have seen so far in America.

Q. What do you like about it?

A. Fountain Square. The Carew Tower. The streets.
Garfield Place. The atmosphere. A grain elevator I
saw on the way in. The Station. The Cincinnati Club.
That little new church. The attitude of the people.
Well dressed. Happy. Larfing. The air is invigorating.
I told you all this before!

Q. What important body of water have you so far
not, to your knowledge, seen?

A. The Ohio River.

Q. Why not?

A. Darkness. Sore feet. Fear of empty streets and
sudden floods. Fear of walking around too much lest
someone think I was sauntering about with the purpose of committing a felony. Hunger. Lack of interest.

Q. What do you like about this part of Ohio?

A. The country is more rolling. Fine long views,
towards the sky, glaring brightness in the west, under
the blowing rain clouds. Fine farms. All over Ohio
you see miles all around: it is all but flat, but not

quite. Trees on the horizon seem to be cities, smoke-stacks—you can't tell. The view of the city from the station, down the long sweep of that avenue. The lighting on the high buildings, at night. Palms on the altars of the churches, for Palm Sunday. The voice of a Jesuit giving absolution to somebody else, in a confessional—and I myself on my way to make a retreat with the Trappists at Gethsemani.

PART 4

Interlude:
Abbey of Our Lady of Gethsemani
[HOLY WEEK, 1941]

¶ I should tear out all the other pages of this book, and all the other pages of anything else I have ever written, and begin here.

This is the center of America. I had wondered what was holding the country together, what has been keeping the universe from cracking in pieces and falling apart. It is places like this monastery—not only this one: there must be others.

Abraham prayed to the Lord to spare Sodom if there should be found in it ten just men. The Blessed Mother of God, the Queen of Heaven and of the Angels, shows Him daily her sons here, and because of their prayers the world is spared, from minute to minute, from the terrible doom.

This is the only real city in America—and it is by itself, in the wilderness.

It is an axle around which the whole country blindly turns, and knows nothing about it. Geth-

semani holds the country together the way the under-
lying substrata of natural faith that goes with our
whole being and can hardly be separated from it,
keeps living on in a man who has "lost his faith"—
who no longer believes in Being and yet himself *is*, in
spite of his crazy denial that He Who IS mercifully
allowed him to *be*.

What *right* have I to be here?

I feel like a thief and a murderer who has been put
in jail and condemned for stealing and murdering all
my life, murdering God's grace in myself and in
others, murdering Him in His image. I have broken
out of the jail in which I lay justly condemned and
have rushed even into the place of the King Whose
Son I murdered, and I implore the mercy of the
Queen who sits here enthroned. . . .

April 8, 1941

OUR LADY OF GETHSEMANI

Paradisus Claustralis.

¶ Abbeys are paradises, in two different senses. That they are at the same time earthly (material) and spiritual (heavenly) paradises is the fruit of a paradox. They are both only because they are purgatories.

What sort of thing is a purgatory? The souls in the real, not analogical, purgatory, are burned by much the same fire as the souls in hell, but the difference is that they bear this burning with love and not with hatred, for they know that through this fire they come to God, Who is all their desire. The souls in hell hate God. Again, the souls in hell know that their pains are just, and hate them all the more for that reason. But the souls in purgatory love not their pains, but the justice of their pains, because they love God's justice, that is, love to do His Will, no matter what it costs them.

To love God is to be like Him. To want to love

185

Him perfectly is to want to be most like Him. To realise how little we actually do love Him, and how unlike Him we really are, is the source of the greatest unhappiness, is the ontological root of all suffering, including the sufferings of hell, where the whole thing is complicated by the fact that the souls even do their best to hate their salvation, which is the likeness to God.

A purgatory is a place where we tear away our sins like plasters although not as suddenly. We do this not for the love of the pain, but in order to get the plasters off, and that hurts.

But there is this paradox: an abbey is an earthly paradise because it is an earthly purgatory.

But if we only love the earthly, or social, or cultural aspect of an abbey, or any other spiritual society (including the Church), it eventually ceases to be any kind of a paradise at all. This abbey is full of cleanness and order and stability in the physical and social order. It is an excellently well-ordered kind of society, and all the surroundings and all the material products of this society are good and pleasing: I mean the buildings and the farm and the orchards and the barns and the church and so on. All, of course, were built and are cared for by the monks. But all these things are not for the monks or any-

body else to enjoy, taking "enjoy" in its proper sense.
For in that sense of enjoyment (*frui*), only God can
be enjoyed, because only God is in Himself the end of
all desire, and not a means to some other end, and you
cannot enjoy anything except the last end of all
desire, in which all is fulfilled.

Even the uses of this material paradise are limited.
You cannot use material things directly to save your
soul, only indirectly. You cannot use a beautiful
church to save your soul, except by praying in it: you
use prayers to save your soul, and prayer may or may
not be easier in one church than in another, depend-
ing largely on you yourself. And their church, here,
is not so much beautiful as it is holy: many people
have really prayed here, and that gives the church
a character beyond its outward beauty.

Again, a bed is used for sleeping on. If the bed
is of boards and the mattress of straw and husks, you
are not using boards and straw to save your soul, but
only to sleep on. If you are doing this out of self-
denial, then it is self-denial you are using to save your
soul, and not a straw mattress. That is why everybody who sleeps on a straw mattress does not thereby
necessarily save his soul.

Again, if you merely deny yourself, you do not save
your soul, because only one thing can save anybody's

soul—the love of God. If you love God in such a manner that the thing you happen to use for sleeping on is no more than a straw mattress, that is all right. It is one of the accidental characters of your own particular love of God, where prayer is more important than sleep.

But how does it happen that this Abbey is an earthly paradise? Work is an important part of the Trappist's life: it is a mixture of penance and recreation. But however hard it is, is still a form of play. Even the strictest penance is a form of play, and especially the Liturgy is play.

"To be as little children" means, for one thing, to do things not because they are strictly necessary, but freely, and out of love; and behind the strictness of the Trappist discipline is this complete metaphysical freedom from physical necessity that makes the whole discipline, ontologically speaking, a kind of play. This making use of work, and penance as play, to save one's soul, results, indirectly, in the abbey being a kind of earthly paradise. The work necessarily produces results, and the results, in this case, are a perfect community, a marvelous farm, beautiful gardens, a fine church, wonderful bread, cheese, butter, all of which make this Abbey at the same time a holy place and one of the best communities, or societies in the earthly sense, in the country. Where, save in a place like this, could one find an example of the truly good "city"?

This accident of Trappist discipline: that it also produces an excellent material result testifies to the goodness of the kind of culture they had in the Middle Ages, no matter what the faults of that time were supposed to be.

The Cistercian monastery results from a combination of the Benedictine Rule, Christian spirituality, and the techniques of living of an agricultural and feudal society. But this isn't merely medieval. There is no trace of any feudalism left, in this Abbey, except perhaps that it feeds the poor of the whole region. Otherwise, it is still a perfect combination of the Benedictine rule and agrarian culture. As long as Christian monasticism and agriculture exist, and they must always exist, this combination of them will be fruitful, and produce societies that are perfect in the same way as this. There is nothing out of date about this Abbey at all.

However, once this is remarked on, you have to go on and say that all the beauty and material excellence of the monastery is only an accident, and their importance and value are only secondary, and relatively trivial. Anyone who comes to the monastery

189

only for its beauty, like those who go to High Mass for the music, are bound to be deceived and betrayed and, eventually, disappointed. The religious life exists and thrives not in buildings or dead things or flowers or beasts but in the soul. And there it exists not as a "good feeling" but as a constant purpose, an unending love that expresses itself now as patience, now as humility, now as courage, now as self-denial, now as justice, but always in a strong knot of faith and hope, and all of these are nothing but aspects of one constant deep desire, charity, love.

Church windows and hymns cannot satisfy us all the time, or even seem to. If they seemed to, what a dangerous deception it would be, because then we would take them for God, who alone can end and fulfill all desire and all longing in peace!

OUR LADY OF GETHSEMANI

"Write my words in thy heart and think diligently on them; for they will be very necessary in the time of temptation.
"What thou understandest not when thou readest, thou shalt know in the day of visitation." THE IMITATION OF CHRIST, III-3-5.

¶ Sometimes we see a kind of truth all at once, in a flash, as a whole. We grasp it in a block, in its wholeness, but not in its details. We see its whole perspective, and as long as this truth stands vividly before us, we contemplate it and seem to understand it. We do not understand it at all thoroughly, yet we know it with some certainty, although vague, rough, and in outline. This is especially true of philosophical and religious ideas.

But once this general figure has become our property and, we think, part of us, in this first easy-seeming intuition, and we store it in our minds and take it for granted, then, by a new series of minute, difficult, toilsome steps we begin to find out, elaborately and with a great deal of trouble, different things that

are only details of this same big idea, and aspects of
it, and parts of it. Thus after seeming to catch the
whole idea at once, easily, we go over the whole
thing again and rediscover it with great difficulty in
all its parts. And this may take months or even years.

We never really begin to understand the idea
until this more arduous and discouraging process
gets under way and, in this process, we seem to live
the idea, working it out in our own experience in the
manner appropriate to our own sad, contingent and
temporal state where nothing is possessed except
successively, in scraps and in pieces.

Yet we always long to possess truth as it is in the
Mind of God, *"tota, perfecta, simul,"* and He sometimes gives intuitions that seem to imitate, in their
completeness, His own knowledge, but their function
is to lead us really to know what we think we know
from these intuitions, by making them more complete
in our own grubbing and rag-picking fashion, after
the first intuition. So we sit and think, like men whose
houses have burned down grubbing in the ashes for
something that might have been saved, until we find
some diamond that had been buried in the wall for
centuries . . .

The same process happens in another way.

At first we see some idea, in block, in general: but

do not even think we understand it. It is a big riddle.
Piece by piece, in our tribulations, we gather up
ideas that seem to have no reference to anything else,
much, until we eventually find that they all have
reference to each other, and the whole complex of
references together make up the answer to this riddle,
which now becomes clear. As for these fragments, we
don't know if we found them by looking for them
(how do we know what to look for?), but they seemed
to turn up in our way and we stumble over them as
if by some curious purpose. They seem to have been
put there for us to find.

The same process, the same pattern of development
holds good for a big image in a poet's mind, a big
figure, a big analogy, big enough to be the subject of
a whole poem, or a *Hamlet*. This image confronts the
poet for years. He may work it out, once, simply, in
one poem, and then work it over and over again in
more complex poems, piece by piece, developing and
complicating metaphors that are all part of one big,
central metaphor.

Andrew Marvell's imagery is all pretty much of one
parcel, and Coleridge's too, but there is more than
just *The Garden* or *The Ancient Mariner* to all their
other poems. But Marvell's best poems are the development of a few big central figures into all their con-

stituent images, seen from a lot of different aspects.

Wordsworth does it. There is a series of poems of
his, from "Lines left on a seat under a yew tree"
through "Tables turned," and "Ode to Duty," to
"Resolution and Independence." The whole group
is a series of attempts to work out the features of one
big idea, which he finally succeeds in doing in the
last one, after making an awful mess of it in all the
others.

This same pattern applies to the development, in
us, of religious experience and spiritual consolations,
which is what Thomas à Kempis happens to be
talking about.

The life of this Abbey is not really understandable
if you only get up at Low Mass—that is, at four a.m.
—because then it is not really clear how the high
point of the day, the center of the day, its religious
noon is the conventual High Mass at 8.

The High Mass is the center and foundation and
meaning of the day here. It *is* the day.

But unless you have been up for six hours, through
all of Matins and Lauds and Low Mass and Prime,
High Mass still seems only the beginning of the day,
and the prelude to something else more significant.
Casting around in our minds for comparisons from

the world, where money-making has to be, they think, the most important thing, we still confusedly imagine that High Mass is only a prelude to work, which is nothing but a kind of recreation by comparison.

It is shocking to see how unprepared we are to understand this, coming from the world where, even if we are not sweating at something we hate merely to get money out of it, anyway we are working for our own good and our own profit, in some sense, all day long, and Mass for the tiny gang that does go daily is still only a prelude to something else!

We find ourselves still assuming that the Mass is only a prelude to something else: penance, mortification, study, anything, so long as the day gets balanced according to the standards of the world, with the main part of it devoted to ourselves. But here the whole meaning of the day is founded on the Passion of Christ. The Mass is the real center, and life is ordered as it should be.

¶ As soon as we know ourselves even a little, we
necessarily become humble—or at least we are
humbled! As soon as we know ourselves, we know our
contingency and our dependence. To know this, to
accept this, is to become humble. Pride always resists
this truth, and tries to make us believe we are the
cornerstone of the universe. Our dependence is a hard
truth to grasp, but the more firmly we grasp it, the
more truly we become humble. We tend rather to
desire our own satisfaction, to center ourselves
entirely upon ourselves, and thus to rebel against
God. To say we are born in sin, is to say we are born
in illusion and blindness, and this blindness makes
us fall into every other evil.

But if we begin to see, we begin to see our dependence, and to see Him on whom we depend. We

begin then to turn to Him, and we seek to learn, no
longer from ourselves but from Him, from His world,
from the Reality which reflects Him all around
us. We turn away from the illusion of ourselves, as
we want ourselves to be, and we begin to accept ourselves as we are and the world as it is.

We must long to learn the secret of our own
nothingness (not God's secret first of all, but our
own secret). But God alone can show us our own
secret. Once we see it, we can seek to receive His love
into our hearts, and we can desire to become like Him.
Indeed, by His love we can begin to become like
ourselves—that is we can find our own true selves, for
we are made in His image and likeness.

God teaches us in tribulations. The most unfortunate people in the world are those who know no tribulations. The most unhappy men are really the ones
who are able to bribe their way out of suffering
and tribulation, and to evade the issue, in pleasures,
in wars, in devotion to a cause like Nazism—which is
moral suicide.

"If I wash thee not, thou shalt have no part in me,"
says Christ to Peter. If Christ does not serve us, that
is put Himself in some way below us, we cannot

live. His humility is greater than ours: He gives us everything—the sun, the light, the pure air, the blossoming fruit trees. He gives us ourselves.

The country here is very beautiful—a wide valley, rolling, dipping land, woods, cedars, dark green fields —grain beginning to come up, perhaps wheat. The monastery barns, the vineyard near the guest-house. The knoll with the statue of St. Joseph on top of it, where the road goes through a shallow cut towards the station, which is on the line from Louisville to Atlanta.

Through the window comes the smell of "full fields"— *odor agri pleni.*

The sun today was as hot as Cuba. Tulips in the front garden have already opened their chalices too wide and have gone blowsy. The bees were at work, one in each flower's cup, although it is still only April. Apple trees are in blossom, and every day more and more buds come out on the branches of the tall trees of the avenue before the gatehouse.

Trappist brothers in their medieval hoods, and heavy home-made boots, tramp along in a line through the vineyard. Bells ring in the steeple.

What all the Spring I had looked forward to finding, when I started from St. Bonaventure, is here,

198

and I haven't been looking at it—for fear of taking
out title deeds and claiming I owned it, for fear of
being possessive with this, as with everything else:
for fear of devouring it like a feast, making a party
out of it—and so losing it.

This morning after Mass, I walked along the wall
of the guest-house garden under the branches of
the fruit trees, in the hot sun, in the midst of more
beauty than I can remember since I was in Rome. I
remember Rome a lot, here.

Then I went inside to the cloister. There the monks
washed the feet of some poor men, put money in their
hands, kissed their hands and feet, gave them a dinner.
I had been afraid at first to see this, thinking it
might prove false. Instead, I saw Christ washing the
feet of Peter. The monks had heard Christ and were
doing what He had told them to do—not a series of
empty gestures but a living liturgical action. I never
knew charity could be spelled out so simply, so in-
nocently, without facade or complication. Christ
spoke, in that act, and made me know Him better and
love Him more—and that is all I seek, in this
place.

❡ "Man when he was in honor, did not understand:
he hath been compared to senseless beasts, and made
like to them." Psalm 48:21.

If we are willing to accept humiliation, tribulation
can become, by God's grace, the mild yoke of Christ,
His light burden. *Onus meum leve.*

This is the feast of our treachery. The rattle makes
its terrible clatter in the cloister. The tabernacle is
empty and lies open. It is as though the winds of
death blew right through us. Our heart is abandoned
to itself, not so much through God's will, as through
our own. He first loved us that we might love Him.
We abandoned Him, He did not abandon us. Because we abandoned Him—His only revenge is to
let us remember that we are alone: this not to be
revenged on us, but to remind us to return to Him.

"I became the most humble and the most abject of
men, that thou mightest overcome thy pride by my

humility," says the Lord, in the words of the
Imitation of Christ.

It is not enough to study Christ's life with the
intention of imitating Him. He must give Himself to
us, He must live in us, He must be humble in us.
Before we can understand the pattern of life that is
given us in Him, we must receive Him, that He
may be life in us. Hence the Cross—for by His
death on the Cross and by the Sacrament of the
Eucharist He gives Himself entirely to us to be our
life.

¶ Charity and freedom are inseparable. Love must be free. Only charity is perfectly free. Love is loved for itself, not determined by anything else outside itself. It is not drawn by the satisfaction of anything less than itself. Only in charity, that is disinterested love, is love perfectly spontaneous.

All love that is less than charity ends in something less than itself. Perfect charity is its own end, and is therefore free, not determined by anything else. God alone is perfectly free, infinitely free. He is Love Loving Himself. Because He is absolutely free, His love can do whatever it likes.

We are constituted in His image by *our* freedom—which is not absolute, but contingent. That is, we are free in proportion as we share His freedom, which is absolute. We are free in the sense that no one determines our free choices: we are so much our own

202

masters that we can even resist God, as we know to
our sorrow! But we are also free to love for the sake
of loving, to love God because He is Love, and to
find ourselves in the perfect freedom of Love's own
giving of itself.

Pride and self-love are the love of death, because
they turn away from God in Whom is all life:
they necessarily tend to non-being, and to death.

Now the sun is setting. Birds sing. Lent is over. I
am tired. Tomorrow is Easter, and I go, for no good
reason, to New York. Out there a couple of blue-
jays are fighting in a tree. I wonder if I have learned
enough to pray for humility. I desire only one
thing: to love God. Those who love Him, keep His
commandments. I only desire to do one thing: to
follow His will. I pray that I am at least beginning
to know what that may mean. Could it ever possibly
mean that I might some day become a monk in this
monastery? My Lord, and my King, and my God!

April 18, 1941

DOUGLASTON, LONG ISLAND

¶ Leaving Gethsemani was sad.

After Benediction on Easter Sunday, in the afternoon, the Church was practically empty. It was very quiet. Sun streamed in on the floor. I made the Stations of the Cross and wished I were going to stay—wished I were able to do so.

I left early Monday morning, got to Louisville at 8. This would have been the middle of the day, at the Abbey—not its beginning. It was confusing. What a difference between the monastery and the outside world! Louisville is a nice enough town, but I was not happy to be thrown back into it.

The world is beautiful with warm sunlight, but the objects in the sunlight are not so beautiful—only strange. Candy in a drug-store window. Newspapers (the Germans are landing in Egypt). Mannequins in

204

store windows. Women's clothes have military in-
signia all over them, now. Speech is violent and hard.
How different to hold on to what I had down there,
at the monastery!

PART 5

*St. Bonaventure, Harlem, and
Our Lady of the Valley*

¶ *Words culled like horrible flowers from a page of
George Eliot:*

bad odor; disgusted; licensed curate; catarrhs; bilious;
"a soup tureen gives a hint of the fragrance that will
presently rush out to inundate your hungry senses";
"the delicate visitation of atoms" (smell);
dinner-giving capacity; keen gusto; "ill flavoured
gravies and cheaper Marsala"; heavy meat-breakfasts;
whiskers; undertaker; monitor; useful practical
matters; mangold-wurzel; "ugliness past its bloom";
inflamed nose; dyspeptic; peptic; "Mr. Duke turned
rather yellow, which was his way of blushing."

Some dream world, is all I can say.

¶ Rudolf Hess, whom I can't be sure I had ever heard
of before, flew from Augsburg to Glasgow in a
fighter plane and gave himself up to the British.

How did I know, since I have given up reading the
papers? Somebody told me at breakfast when I
had my mouth full of cornflakes, if not Pep.

There were a whole lot of bullets in the tail of his
plane. The story is more romantic if the bullets
were German.

There are certain things I like about this crazy
story.

First, he had never flown a Messerschmitt before.

Second, Hitler had issued special orders that he
wasn't to fly any planes anyway. It is difficult to believe in a government, the head of which issues solemn
orders that another member of the ruling party is not
to be allowed to fly any planes! If the world is to be
turned upside down by such a nursery full of

paranoiacs it really means the end has come, and we will be destroyed, as Swift foresaw, unworthy of fire and brimstone but the target of terrific and ludicrous insults.

He landed by parachute on the estate of a friend in Scotland, and asked for his friend at once, as though he had hit some neutral spot in the midst of the war, a sanctuary in some Scotch living-room. Knowing the Scotch living-rooms of novels, this is easily believable, I suppose.

As soon as he disappeared, the Germans gave out a story that he had gone crazy and done himself in, which was a truly hasty and unhappy thought for a propaganda bureau that is supposed to be fiendishly clever. Of course they are not clever at all: German propaganda wouldn't fool even a German, at any other time but this. But anyway, if they are so smart: why did they say Hess went crazy, and in fact had been off his nut for some time? What? A member of the perfect government, off his nut? Which only goes to show how common the idea is in Germany that the Nazis are lunatics, when even the propaganda bureau tells the truth about them!

Hess was also the most obedient and perfect Nazi. Now I suppose the English are going to glorify him as the "one good Nazi"—as if, having created a "good element" in the Nazi Party, they could now proceed to demonstrate that that "element" was now deserting Hitler. What for? For all his failures in France, Norway, and Greece?

But the one really funny thing about the story is a little incident which, when thought about, has quite interesting implications. I mean something that bears witness to a tiny, private and ascetic drama in Hess' own bettle-browed soul, at the time of his landing in Scotland.

Of course he is a vegetarian, non-smoker, teetotaler. I am not sneering at those people as such. I feel good myself since I don't smoke or drink: but I don't understand people who give up these things just in order to feel good, or just because they think they are immoral. I only understand a man who likes smoking and drinking and doesn't think they are immoral and gives them up because he wants to give them up.

Well, Hess came sailing down into a Scotch field, and a farmer came out and led him home at the point of a hayfork, and Hess was charming and polite and even before he got to the door the farmer's wife was making tea. I guess when the Germans invade England, someone will run inland shouting, "Visitors,

unwelcome, but nevertheless, visitors," and all the
old ladies will start making tea.

But when Hess was offered the tea, "he smiled,"
said the story (which I had to go and read) and
refused, saying "he never drank tea that late."

The fantasy of this part of the story is truly out-
rageous. Imagine the self-conscious and embarrassed
smile of a man who has flown several hundred miles
through a war shot at by his own fighters as well as by
the enemy, landing in the enemy country like Robert
Donat pursued by spies, having dropped through
the darkness in a parachute, and hurt his ankle, now
making this tiny, trivial act of self-denial!*

The conflict of the ascetic context with *The Thirty-
nine Steps* element of the story is shattering!

The problem of an asceticism that is reduced to a
lot of secret and embarrassed private resolutions, de-
tached from any real beliefs, any metaphysics, any
theology, any Charity is all laid out here, as neat as
you could want it, and the whole thing is even
magnified a thousand times by the fact that it also
occurs in this absurd, spy-story context.

And people don't know it, but this is getting to be

---

* Twenty years later. It has just dawned on the author that perhaps
Hess refused the tea because he was afraid it would keep him awake.

one of the more important minor problems of our time. There is, I think, going to be a crazy and half-hearted striving after self-discipline and unsystematic asceticism everywhere. It is going to look very funny indeed, in some of the violent maniacs that will associate it with various murders and other completely fantastic crimes!

Anybody who really does want to deny himself is going to be put to great embarrassment by the numbers of ascetical murderers and self-denying dope fiends that are going to fill the world!

¶ I just thought of Tenterden, Kent. Last I heard of
Tenterden was in Graham Greene's book about
Mexico, where he talked about reading of Tenterden
in Cobbett's *Rural Rides,* while he was in Mexico in
some hot place full of flies. Tenterden had a very
wide street, stands in the Kentish downs, open country, under a fine sky. It also had a fine church tower.
We went there when I was at Rye, when I was fourteen; maybe I took a picture of the church with my
box camera. Greene, sitting in his hot place full of
flies, quoted Cobbett on Tenterden, and Cobbett, removed from me by more than a century, made me see
the same wide street, while I sat tilting this chair I
am sitting on, here in an American monastery, reading
Greene . . .

Greene, under the mosquito netting, in Villahermosa where they burned all the churches, sweating,
listening for the rats, read Trollope. I haven't read

Trollope, but I think of the Cathedral close at
Canterbury, the fine towers, the high trees, the rooks,
the deanery. The deanery always made me feel
strange; to me the one thing worse than being a don
was being a dean.

Greene reads this in Mexico, Tabasco, one of the
worst and hottest provinces, where the churches were
burned flat. I sit in my room in a North American
monastery, and tilt my chair, and look out at the blue
green hills, getting covered with summer, and think
about Canterbury, in the Easter rain and sunshines of
1930. Maybe I'll read Trollope, but I think not. I
also thought maybe I would try Meredith's *The
Egoist* again, since I have to lecture on it tonight. But
no. I don't want to read any novels.

I respect Greene, for reading novels under the
mosquito netting in Villahermosa, especially Trollope. Maybe it was *The Warden* he read, but I forget.
I guess if you read novels, you may be a real novelist.
I can't read novels anymore. That is why I am writing
a journal. Greene's book about Mexico was a
journal. That is the kind of thing I like to read. The
Cuban Journal I wrote was far better than last year's
lousy novel, too.

I am amazed at all the novels I read between the
ages of seventeen and twenty. I was never able to

swallow Hardy, although I read practically everything else, D. H. Lawrence, Stella Benson, Virginia
Woolf, John Dos Passos, Jules Romains, Hemingway,
Balzac, Flaubert, Celine, even some short stories
by Stefan Zweig, some Vicki Baum, and the other
day when I was sitting in the sun I remembered
with embarrassment how I tried to explain to my
godfather why I liked Luciano Zuccoli's bad porno-
graphic novel *La Divina Fanciulla.* I said it was
"very Italian."

I have read enough novels, and I don't want to read
any more. Also, I think the novel is a lousy art
form anyway.

I sat in the Gardens of the Villa Borghese, in 1931,
and read in Italian translation something by Maurice
Dekobra. I must have been nuts.

The next time I was in Rome, I was eighteen, and
was able to read *Ulysses.*

¶ Even if I wanted to write history in this journal I don't know how I could. There is supposed to be a war going on. But you don't know what is happening, what is important, what is unimportant; what is true, what is not; what means your life or death and what doesn't. Even those who think they know what matters are confused about it, and confuse everybody else by their own caution.

Roosevelt and his government all seem to want to help England with everything, navy, army, airplanes and people like me, everything. If they know that is important, however, they feel that they can't convince people of that importance without playing some kind of a trick on them.

Washington is full of weak tricks.

They make speeches on the radio. Maybe a lot of people listen. I haven't listened to any of them, or talked about any of them, so I wouldn't know. But

apparently they make speeches on the radio, and each
speech is supposed to be a little candy-coated pill. The
people swallow the pill, and then the government
watches them to see if they liked it or didn't like it.

But the government has been watching too close,
and the people haven't been reacting right, and
maybe too many haven't been listening to the
speeches, which is probably the most disappointing
thing of all.

All I know is, that if these politicians know what
matters, if they know what is important, they ought to
be able to say so sincerely and convincingly, without
getting scared, hysterical, cagey, obscure, or in some
strange complex way of their own, diplomatic about
it.

If they know what is vital, what is necessary to save
the world, they should be able to say it with some
show of conviction. At least with enough show of
conviction to scare the people who disagree with
them, or to start some kind of a real reaction. But all
that is happening is a series of crazy, futile, artificial
movements across the surface of the country. The land
is being lightly stirred by wind, and everybody more
or less refuses to pay too much attention. It may be a
good thing, and it may be a bad thing, I'm sure I don't
know which.

I was never so convinced of anything as that I haven't any idea what this is all about, what people are doing. I think a lot of people are crazy, and a lot of people just refuse to have anything happen to them, and have become, instinctively, stubborn, in a fairly good, animal sort of a way. They won't be moved.

That is another thing that nobody had expected.

The common rationalization that everybody was handing around before was: "The bands will play and flags wave and you will fall out of the window of your office, you poor sap, in your haste to go and save the world." Well, first, the bands were slow in getting started, and even now the band-playing is pretty timid and disorganised, and the bands are not making such a terrific racket, or a racket that is in the least exciting. The noise of the bands by now is still slightly annoying because of its timidity and its monotony and its confusion.

The other part of the rationalisation is that it had become everybody's property. Everybody knew that the bands would play, everybody knew that everybody else was going to fall for propaganda, everybody was, at the same time, thoroughly unwilling to go to war.

Now they are all sitting around waiting for the propaganda to start, and waiting to not listen to it.

If that is so, that would be the best aspect of the situation. Only that isn't so.

I came across some people in New York who were a lot more keyed up than they were when I last saw them. Girls. Their lipstick was brighter, their dresses fancier, they had hundreds of friends who were in the Army, and they were pretty free with the terms "fifth columnist" and "lousy Nazi," and they used these words with quite a bit of feeling.

But on the other hand, their attitude was just as confused as anybody else's, because another of their phrases, and one that they also used with a lot of strong feeling was that "of course America wouldn't get into it—do you think?"

What these people are is: scared. They are the ones who have been reading all the papers and listening to all the radio reports, and they are excited. Their excitement is not caused by propaganda, exactly, because there has been no exciting propaganda. All the propaganda has been clumsy and equivocal and cautious.

So these people are really living on self-generated excitement of their own, built up from biting their nails in front of the radio. And the thing that makes them most nervous about the radio is not the abundance of scaring news that comes over it, but the fact that the same meager news is all they get five times a day, over and over, on all the successive news broadcasts.

Another weakness in the propaganda, as far as I know, is that it is all built up on completely equivocal guesses about the future or else self-contradictory and incomprehensible statements about the present that nobody can quite grasp.

The big weakness of the propaganda is that it is entirely abstract, and that the people who are uttering it have no firm grasp of abstraction anyway.

There has been no tendency whatever to play up the physically exciting propaganda, horror stuff, blood, cruelty, violence. All the propaganda has been abstract. What is physically violent about the propaganda is all left over from before the war: stories about concentration camps, stormtroopers, brutality, sadism, priests and pastors whipped and clubbed, and so forth.

The bombing of Rotterdam is the most horrible thing that has so far happened, from what I know. There has not been much emphasis on it. It is one of the things that makes me sickest. But all we know about it, aside from wild stories, is the extent of the

physical destruction. We are told that probably so
many millions of dollars worth of property damage
has been done. But who cares about a million dollars
worth of property? That damage is completely abstract anyway.

We are told a little about the people killed. The
stories are terrible. The people were probably killed
in thousands and very painfully. Some of the stories
of general carnage are so picturesque that they sound
false. But Rotterdam has a frightful story, the fright-
fulness of which is only diminished by the unnecessary
picturesqueness of some of the stories that are so grue-
some that they sound like lies.

The general attitude of the people is to refuse to
hear anything of this kind at all. They refuse to listen.
They say it is propaganda before you start.

Catholics in this country don't particularly care
what has happened to the church in Poland. They
don't want to hear anything about it. But the information about the church in Poland is probably completely reliable, since it comes from the Vatican.
Nevertheless, people are just as willing not to hear
that news on the grounds that it is "British propaganda." That is their answer to it. The real reason
why they won't listen is simply that they don't want

to hear anything about suffering. They don't want to hear about the horrors of the war. They don't want to listen.

¶ Outside the walks shine with rain, inside, up the
hall, students play on an accordion and sing, badly. I
just read the last story in *Dubliners,* "The Dead."

It is a curious business, reading a story like that. It
took some effort, to begin with. It is a good story, that
is, it is good writing. But at least the first half of it is
terribly dull, because . . . O, I don't know why. The
story is much too long, perhaps. Beyond the point
where the man makes the corny speech at the party,
it gets good. The arrivals of the guests before the
party are tedious, pretty, smooth, sharp, neat. The end
of the story is very pretty, and I suppose it is the thing
from *Dubliners* that everybody is always quoting, the
very last paragraph, about the snow falling softly
through the universe.

Maybe instead of writing this story, Joyce should
simply have written a poem about the snow falling
through the universe. The business about the dead

227

is, in fact, better material for a poem than it is for a story. Maybe the whole of *Dubliners,* especially "The Dead," is an indication of the fact that the novel as it has been established by the eighteenth century and perfected by the nineteenth is dead. *Ulysses* is a different kind of novel, a journal and a mobile, not a novel. *Finnegan's Wake* is a mobile. "The Dead" is just a tedious, pretty, failure of a story that should have been something else: a poem, or something. *A Portrait of the Artist* is not a novel, but more of a journal.

There are two good novels written in English in the twentieth century or, anyway, there are two good novelists, writing real novels—Richard Hughes and E. M. Forster. If you want to use the word novel to cover practically anything like *Ulysses* or *Of Time and The River,* there are more good novels (and I don't include *Of Time and The River* as especially good). These are novels in some different sense from *Vanity Fair* or *The Egoist.* But novels in the proper sense, I admire, when they are by Hughes or Forster. But I can't see trying to write them.

If it is hard for me to read *Dubliners,* it is impossible for me to imagine writing like that. I tried to this January, and the stories were absurd. When I think of those two stories, and of the fact that I have not yet tossed them into the incinerator, my stomach aches.

It takes more effort for me to read *Dubliners* than anything else by Joyce. I like reading *Ulysses* better than *Finnegan's Wake,* but only a little better. Anyway those are the two books of Joyce's I like to read, and can read without any phony compulsion, any sense of duty, any imposed concentration ("Keep going, maybe it will get interesting later on").

A Portrait of the Artist is a good book, full of neat writing. In *Ulysses* I am beginning to find parts that are slightly embarrassing and, in an obscure way, corny. They are beginning to get dated—that is, they are things that are smart and bright only in a very limited context which is being wiped out.

Finnegan's Wake, in this sense, is Joyce's most universal work, in the sense that it is the most independent, in every respect, of time, changes in fashion, changes in gags, and the prevailing weather of wisecracks, and all those things. To take as an instance of universality in art a work that can be understood by everybody who has never had any interest in art before, nor has now, nor ever will have, is a misuse of the word universality.

Mathematics are universally true. But we do not lay down the law that the mathematician whose

theories are not immediately clear without any effort
of concentration to somebody who barely knows how
to add, should be thrown in jail and no longer be
allowed to think up his obscure theories, being as how
they aren't universal enough.

Some people say that a work of art must be understood at once, and liked immediately, by all, even
those who hate art from the beginning, for it to be
called "universal." The notion of universality, in
this sense, doesn't mean anything at all. Good art is
universal because it is good, not good because it is
universal in some degraded sense: that is, the value
of a work of art is not subservient to the tastes of
people who are simply not interested in art at all.

That would be like demanding that the truth be
able to contradict itself, or saying that God is not
really omnipotent because it is impossible for Him to
do anything that would lessen His own perfection,
and therefore to demand that He be able to contradict Himself, and make Himself, if He should want
to, pure nothingness out of pure actuality.

That is what pious people do, who say that religious
art that does not conform to the tastes of people who
love one particular kind of "prettiness" (because they
have never wanted to love anything else) is not "universal" and therefore not sacred or beautiful.

If a thing has any real beauty, it is universal: that is, its beauty is capable of being seen by everybody if they are willing to humble themselves, and sacrifice their own individual prejudices and bad taste, to come at the beauty they cannot see at first. A work of art is universal not by conforming to the separate prejudices of a whole series of different individuals, but by being simple, accessible to everybody, once they have cast out their sins of prejudiced taste, once their eye is single and their body lightsome.

¶ Baroness de Hueck came and made a speech about Harlem to the nuns and clerics who are here for summer school.

She put her fist on her hip and made a slow gesture with the flat of her other hand and said: "Baloney!" in the middle of the speech somewhere, and knocked all the religious off their chairs.

Afterwards the nuns were very enthusiastic and excited, because nuns are good, and the only reason they didn't already know the things the Baroness had to say is that they had never been told. Unlike some of the priests, they were not ready to resist everything that was said about Charity with certain "prudent" arguments, because the prudence of the world is opposed to God's Charity, but divine prudence, given by the Holy Ghost, cannot conflict with Charity for it *is* Charity. So the Baroness, in going to Harlem and living in voluntary poverty there to work among

232

the poor, is more *prudent* as well as more charitable
than someone who lives in perfect security all his life
doing, without important crises or troubles, a routine
job with mediocre results: but who tends to tell himself all along: "Well, I'm not a saint, but at least
I'm *prudent*." Prudent is too likely to mean
"mediocre."

One of the little nuns walked around all day ear-
nestly startled, full of new ideas, looking as eager as
a child full of the expectancy of going to grandma's in
New Jersey next Sunday. The nuns are swell.

The Baroness had a good easy way of standing up
and talking, and made good, simple, unhysterical
gestures, very natural, and had a strong, sure voice.
Best of all she used the word "martyrdom" without
embarrassment, not like something crazy and "imprudent" and abstract in some old book.

¶ Down in Harlem, at Friendship House, today.

Yesterday, full of *Hail Marys,* I went there. Today I sorted dresses and shoes in the clothing center.

Walking across 135th Street, between the clothing center and the library (where the Baroness has her desk in the window), you see, looking west, City College, on top of the hill, looking very surprised. A big building carrying the letters Y-M-C-A, white upon black. A movie. Seven or eight push-carts. The drabbest billiard parlor in the world. The subway station at the corner of Lenox Avenue. Hundreds of little Negro kids walking by solemnly, holding kites.

A pair of Army trucks go by, full of Negro soldiers, leaning very far out and laughing excitedly at the strangeness of their own race, all along the street. Very fast, the trucks are gone.

I try to call Lax at Godfrey's, on East 18th Street, but the phone has been disconnected. Later I go

234

down, by mistake, to *West* 18th Street and have to cross town on the 23rd Street bus.

Outside Godfrey's in the middle of the night, Roger Beirne made a long, sentimental Mr. Chips speech in the street, very funny, and later he addressed the most resounding business speech, funnier than anything I ever heard, to the darkened offices of the Burroughs Adding Machine Company.

¶ While I was saying prayers in St. Patrick's Cathedral,
I saw Harlem standing afar off like the publican:
*"Stans a longe publicanus, nolebat oculos ad caelum
levare . . ."* The publican, who did not even dare
look up to heaven!

Then gentle, ragged kids are running fast through
the dark warrens of the tenements and out into the
street. A mother cries out to one of them: "Don't fly
your kite on the roof! Don't go up there to fly your
kite. It will drag you away!"

The other day I went to the Baroness' place for
the first time. At first I didn't find anybody around
who was in charge of anything. But in the bookstore
there were half a dozen highschool kids, or maybe
they were old enough for college, if it makes sense
to talk about Negroes being of college age when it
isn't possible for most of them to go to a college.

Anyway they were sitting around a table having an

argument about something. It went like this: One
would say, "Well I don't think that's right," and
everybody would burst out laughing. Then another
would say: "Well I *do* think that's right," and they
would all burst out laughing again. They were very
happy, and it didn't matter much what they were
arguing about. I'm sure that's the best kind of argument to have, anyway, happy.

Today I was in the clothing room for the afternoon,
sorting shoes.

Last night some little kids gave a play, for the
Baroness' birthday. The play was very complicated
and funny, and every line was chanted in a shrill
monotone with pauses in the wrong places where the
prompter's voice came out in a big whisper. They had
rifled the clothing room for very fantastic costumes,
and the spectacle was one of the most amazing I ever
saw. It was on a little stage in the back of an empty
store used as a kids' clubroom.

The story was about King Arthur and his Knights,
and was a comedy written for amateur performance
by suburban high schools. The jokes about the
country club, the golf course, the pink tea party, took
on a curious ambiguity spoken by these kids in this
store crowded with their poor and silent and perplexed parents. Every time anybody said "country

club" I wanted to beat my head against a wall, it was
so terrible. It was as though these innocent kids were
spelling out a prophecy of the Last Judgment, without
knowing what they were saying, condemning by
their own complete innocence and ignorance of the
stupidities they were talking about, all the injustice
that had fallen upon them and their parents' parents,
for generations!

Otherwise, it was a very funny play, artfully funny.
They knew when they were doing something good,
and made sure what good jokes there were came out
better than the author of the play would ever have
been able to imagine them. But the goodness of the
whole thing was just the kind of goodness the author
wouldn't have been capable of wanting: they had the
sort of sophistication you get in some medieval mys-
tery play—the medievalism was all in their own innocence, not in any idea of the author's at all, and they
had none of the fake smoothness and glibness that
they were supposed to have. The play was at the
same time naïve and stilted and full of good gestures,
and so it was perfect.

¶ *"You for your part can draw up a new code of laws,
a plan of a new socialist state, and I for mine will
give my coat to a beggar: and until you have given
your own coat to the poor and shared your own bread
with those who starve, your code and your planned
society are liable to be jokes,"* say the prophets and
the saints.

If you first become, yourself, voluntarily poor, then
you may perhaps learn something about laws to help
the poor: but you have to become poor out of true
Charity, that is, the Love of God.

There are no such things as charitable laws, but
only charitable people. A law is as good as the people
who keep it, and no matter how just a law is, it will
be a joke if all the people under the law, or enforcing
it, are unjust and avaricious.

Our society is diseased with our own selfishness and

239

avarice. It is no great trick to know that society is
sick. Everybody can offer you some kind of reason
why it is: The laws are all wrong. The government
is all wrong. There ought to be laws against grafters.
And one group of people who are interested in nothing else but money try to pass a law controlling the
avarice of another group of people just like themselves. Then they wonder why the law doesn't do any
good.

We refuse to love our neighbors, and excuse ourselves on the ground that the laws are supposed to
take care of all that, or that the revolution will, if
the laws can't.

Social Security does not make it unnecessary for me
to feed the poor, and if nobody loves the poor, and
nobody will sacrifice himself to feed them, the Social
Security Law will never help anybody.

Nevertheless, it is better that there should be such
laws than that there should be no humanitarian laws
at all: and if I know this, and like the law and vote
for the kind of men who make it and try to persuade
others to get more laws passed like this, that is so
natural that it isn't even worth comment: that makes
me no kind of a hero that I can think of. When I have
done all that I have still done nothing. And if I have
done all that, voted for Social Security and at the same

time thought of nothing much, the rest of the time, but my own profit, I have just wasted my time. I might just as well be on the side of those who frankly hate everything that takes the least amount of profit away from them, and also hate Social Security and every other law that gives something to somebody but themselves.

No law will ever abolish poverty.

No revolution will ever abolish poverty.

Poverty will never be abolished as long as everybody loves riches, or honors, or position, or fame, or importance.

Poverty will never be abolished unless the whole world becomes voluntarily poor, which does not appear likely, right this minute. So maybe, instead, we will be destroyed by fire from heaven.

But there is one thing certain: those who pretend they love God, and pray to Him, and even receive His Body and Blood sacrificed entirely for them in the Eucharist, and still hate laws which are meant to help feed the poor and clothe the needy and care for the sick, had better look to their consciences, and see whether the reason they hate the law isn't that they themselves fear to lose some of their profits if such laws go through!

Everybody knows that there isn't a man in the world who will admit he hates a measure because it "will help the poor." We all argue that the legislation we don't like will not only *not* help the poor but wreck the whole country: that is why we fear it.

Such people are not incapable of finding out, by examining their consciences, whether or not, when they say that, they are lying to themselves!

September 3, 1941

OUR LADY OF THE VALLEY, R. I.

"Nam quantum unusquisque est in oculis tuis, tantum est et non amplius, ait Sanctus Franciscus." IMITATION OF CHRIST, III-50

¶ What we are, our identity, is only truly known to God, not to ourselves, and not to other men.

So the greatest terror of the particular judgment will be, that the moment after death we shall instantly appear before the face of God and learn our true identity: see who we really are! What we have made of ourselves!

The measure of our identity, or our being (for here the two mean exactly the same thing) is the amount of our love for God. The more we love earthly things, reputation, importance, ease, success and pleasures, for ourselves, the less we love God. Our identity gets dissipated among a lot of things that do not have the value we imagine we see in them, and we are lost in them: we know it obscurely by the way all these things disappoint us and sicken us once we get what

243

we have desired. Yet still we bring ourselves to nothing, annihilate our lives by trying to fulfill them on things that are incapable of doing so. When we really come to die, at last, we suddenly know how much we have squandered and thrown away, and we see that we are truly annihilated by our own sick desires: we were nothing, but everything God gave us we have also reduced to nothing, and now we are pure death.

Then most of all, by the light of Pure Being, does such nothingness become horrible. No one knows how to describe how something that is almost nothing retains enough being (since we are immortal) to feel the anguish of its own nothingness forever.

But if we have loved God all our lives and lost ourselves in Him, seeming to die to the things of the world, we find ourselves again in Him, perfected and live forever in joy.

Tribulation detaches us from the things that are really valueless, because their attraction cannot stand up under it, and all satisfactions that are meaningless appear as such when we are filled with tribulation. Therefore we should be grateful for it if God sends us tribulations and sorrows, because they help us love Him by destroying the value of the things that are insufficient to fulfill our love. And the reason we

244

suffer under this tribulation is, as St. John of the
Cross says, that we have let go of the goods that can
no longer please us, while the one thing we most
love is not yet given to us: so for the time being we
have nothing, and only ache with the sense of our
own poverty.

Pray for that kind of sorrow!

¶ A people that loves peace only because war is horrible, degrading, unprofitable and extremely filthy and revolting, is very likely to get mixed up in a war quite soon, and also, to get beaten in it. No matter how horrible anything is, that we can bring about by our own wills, there has to be some better reason for avoiding it than merely that it is physically "horrible."

Since the last war, people have hated war mostly because of the filthiness of the trenches, the agony of the wounded and the mutilated, the horrible fate of the crippled, and all the physically disgusting side of the war. That is natural enough. But they have also made the mistake, in many places, of believing that because they themselves were horrified, by this, everybody else also felt the same: and if that was so, nobody would ever want to go to war again. The craziness of that belief is quite obvious, today. It is

not even true that the German soldiers went to war
unwillingly. In many cases they tore into Poland and
France with the most barbarous enthusiasm.

Another favorite reason for not going to war was
that it wasn't profitable, didn't "get you anything,"
but on the contrary only produced "another depression." This is another wrong reason, one that is
irrational as well as immoral, for hating war, because
it assumes that the most important thing in the world
is material prosperity, and that a war could not possibly have any result whose value might be more important than the difficulties of a depression to pay for
it.

It is entirely useless to point out that if the fear of
depression is not enough to make war totally unde-
sirable, it is an even more immoral reason for actually
going to war. "If Hitler wins, we will all be ruined."

Fighting is a question involving morality, and the
material profitableness of certain actions has nothing
to do with their moral goodness or evil.

That war is horrible and also (at present, to capitalist society) possibly ruinous, is certainly no reason
for saying it is immoral. If this war is immoral and
unjust, somebody had better find some better reasons
than these for saying so. The morality of this war is
no question I can pretend to settle. The reason I

think that those who want America to go to war with
Germany eventually (only idiots want us to get in
right away) are wrong, is that none of their arguments
for going in are very relevant either.

A. MacLeish used to express all the old arguments
against war: it is horrible, and we fool ourselves if we
think it is "getting us anything." Now that he has
seen that there must be something wrong with these
arguments, he has reversed his position, but he has
done so in such a way as to make us twice as suspicious
of anything he says, because what he says now is just
as bad as what he used to attack. Now, side-stepping
the question of the horrors of war, he turns around
and says that it is not true that war cannot "save
democracy." It *can*. In other words, he has just gone
back to the slogans he had successfully pointed out
before to be a little too glib and general to have much
meaning.

It seems to me beyond question that, if we enter
this war and even if we don't, our particular culture
(democracy) is bound to be fundamentally changed.
Maybe so much so that it will be unrecognizable. In
any case, what phase of that culture is MacLeish talking about? We will never get back the nineteen
twenties, and nobody should want to either. Maybe
that is what the ordinary person thinks of as "democ-

racy," the transitory state of prosperity when absolutely everybody could own a Stutz.

For those who want to get into the war, I think
their position would sound a lot more honest in some
such terms as these:

"It is true that the war is terrible and it will probably wreck us, economically and politically, even if
we stay out. If we go in, it is going to cost us many
lives, as well as all our money, because there is no use
pretending our Army won't have to fight, since we
intend to wipe out Germany. (Of course Roosevelt
is still hypocritically holding up his hands in horror
at the thought that any life will be lost.) However,
all these horrors must be endured if we are ever going
to have a real peace afterwards—that is, a peace
where certain fundamental human values will be
respected, and where it will be possible to reconstruct
some kind of a fairly just social order.

"Obviously if Hitler wins (and I don't deny this
myself) there will be at best a joke of an armistice,
followed by chaos and trouble all over the world for
two hundred years, in which life will be almost unbearable for everybody including Germans, and if
there is 'order' anywhere, it will respect no real
human or spiritual values at all.

"On the other hand, if we go into this war and

succeed in destroying Hitler and his armies, there will
be peace and a new order. We may lose what we now
call democracy, and all thought of economic security,
but at least fundamental rights will be in some way
respected even while the new order is built. At least
there will be some freedom left: perhaps no freedom
of the press, or of expression, but a man will not
actually be enslaved, which is something. It will be
worth losing so many things, if only we can remove
the menace of that intolerable disregard of all values
from the face of the earth."

If all this is true, and if going to war is the only way
we can safeguard some chance of peace and order in
the world afterwards, the war is not unjustifiable.
But the argument is an old one. In fact, it is Hitler's
argument, turned around. He says that there can be
no peace until the capitalist empires have been wiped
out. . . . Of course he says so in such a way that it
is quite clear he is planning no just order, but a complete German tyranny, frankly built up on the en-
slavement of the conquered peoples. This is no hysterical metaphor. Slavery is exactly what he plans, for
as many as he can actually enslave. The others will be
dominated by starvation or, at least, a relentless
economic and military pressure.

The big catch in our argument is the promise that if *we* won there would be peace and order in the world.

That is the whole trouble. What kind of order?

Everything that has been said by Roosevelt or Churchill or anybody else demonstrates with a terrifying clearness that they have absolutely no idea at all of any definite new order in the world. They have only the vaguest and most muddled notion of what exists for them to do. All they do is mumble that "we must win." After that, their minds are a complete blank. They do not even seem able to imagine some of the things a British and American victory involves. If they are going to police the world, it means keeping on foot a colossal Army and Navy for years, and it means being able to sit on the world the way Hitler intends to sit on it. Obviously there is only one Hitler now, and if we become as bad as he is later (which doesn't look probable), there is not much advantage, for the world at large, in our winning this war.

However, if this is to be decided as a moral question, it must involve everybody's advantage, and not just two empires'.

Most of all, they talk as if the same economic structure and the same social structure we have now would survive the war. Indeed, that is taken for granted. That is perhaps the most dangerous of all their suppositions.

The present capitalist system has got certain terrific weaknesses which, if it survives the war at all, which it may, will make inevitable a series of revolutions that will be almost as bad as a German victory: and that is clearly not something to die for! Especially since one of the results of these revolutions may be an "order" something like Nazism or Fascism or the Dictatorship of the Proletariat, but most probably Fascism, in this country.

Maybe that is why our war aims are so ridiculous and so confused. If they were any more objective, any more frank, the only conclusion would be this: all we will be fighting for in the end will be to make possible an American revolution, followed by Fascism, instead of letting ourselves be controlled by a Nazi empire. If that is so, it may turn out a little more pleasant for a minority of Americans. But as a whole it doesn't give a moral solution to the problem of this war for the whole world, or even an advantageous one for most of us in America.

[Note twenty years later: I have allowed this long passage to be reproduced *in extenso* not because I think it is particularly wise and certainly not because

I think it presents a prophecy that has been "fulfilled." There may, of course, be some truth in it somewhere. But in any case, this is the way very many people were thinking *before* Pearl Harbor. And most of us have probably forgotten what a big change can be made by a single incident in history.]

¶ Today I walked about in the dry grass of the tank-lots, where it was very warm, warm as summer. Yet many of the trees and bushes were already bare and leaves flew in the warm wind. The hills were full of color, and the sky had in it piles of white cumulus cloud—I forget where I thought I had seen a sky exactly like that before.

In any case, I was sorry it was hot, and glad it was going to be Fall—glad to see through the trees. There is a severer and stricter beauty about bare woods. This appeals to me sometimes more than anything summer brings to the country.

Really, I like every season, and the season I like best is the one I am in at the time. I like all the seasons best, in turn, one after the other—but one I do get tired of: winter.

A silly little red cub plane came skidding clumsily

over the trees and bounced down into a field near
where I was sitting. Instantly a man and a dog sprang
up from nowhere and ran to it. It was so much like
a rendezvous of spies that I did not go near. Five
minutes later, running men arrived through the fields
from every part of the landscape, thinking there had
been an accident.

I went back and sat down where I was before.
Presently the sky filled with fancy grey clouds of the
kind that were carefully, dramatically, and realis-
tically painted by the artists of the 19th century.

¶ Once there was a man who became very rich during
the armaments boom and he said to himself: "All
this money embarrasses me for several reasons. First,
I don't like the idea of having made a fortune out of
war in which millions of people are being killed. But,
second, even if the way I had made this money did not
make me feel dirty all over, even if I had made this
money out of producing something useful, that would
make people happier, even then, I have so much
money that I have to get rid of it—it embarrasses me!

"What will I do? Perhaps I will spend it on a good
time. But strangely enough, all the pleasures of the
society I live in have begun to bore me, they seem so
empty. They even make me feel a little sick. I spit
out the very thought of them, they embarrass me as
much as the money itself. I don't want pleasure any
more than I want this money.

"What will I do, then? Buy a better house, and

better cars, and records, and pianos, and books, and paintings, and live like a cultured and comfortable person? But I am satisfied with what I have already, and I do not really want more expensive satisfactions, any more than I want this money. They all embarrass me.

"Of course, I might put the money away for a rainy day, in case something might happen to me—I might need it. But there is so much more than I would ever need, that there would always be too much left over. Of course, I could give it to hospitals and clinics, but the country is already full of hospitals and clinics. And why give it to "charity"? That is just a matter of signing a check and handing it to someone who passes it on to somebody else who sends it to the bank, and when a cut has been taken out for the one who got the check out of me, and another check cut for this agent, and another for that one, it will finally get to those who need it, but only after they have been put through the third degree to see if they are really *poor enough* to have some of it. Besides, I would get my name in the papers, and would have to pay that much less income tax, and so forth, and this too would make me feel cheap.

"I know what I will do. I will go down into the part of the city where everything is terrible, and where everyone is having a hard time, and I will give money directly to the people who need it. I will spend it myself for those who need clothes and food. I will go where everything is ugly and evil as death, and I will live there myself, and I will share all that I have with the people who live there, and they can have all the money I make except for what I need to keep going myself."

So then the man took all the money he had and gave it directly to the people in the worst part of the city, without asking any questions, just giving his money to everybody who was sick and down and out and starving. And after he had no more money left, he was one of them himself. In this way he got rid of several million dollars.

Is there anyone in the world who would believe such a thing to be possible?

¶ I cannot say I am making much money. I get $45
a month, plus room and board. Yet the life I lead
here is as happy as the richest kind of life and, as far
as I am concerned, just as comfortable. How can I
write about poverty when, though I am in a way poor,
yet I still live as though in a country club?

Why do I ask myself questions all the time about
what I ought to be doing? Why am I always unsatisfied
and asking myself at all times what is my vocation?
Or whether my vocation is to stay here reading, and
praying, and writing, and sometimes teaching a class?

Friday morning. Before we drive up to Buffalo to
meet Catherine de Hueck (who is coming to speak
here)—the following things come clear in my mind:
that she will probably ask me to come to Friendship
House. That if she does, it is not necessarily to be
taken as a sign that I am supposed to go there—that

it is God's will. I wouldn't decide anything before-
hand. Make no decisions until the time for making
decisions. In general, I am tentatively on defence
against going to Friendship House.

¶ Riding to Buffalo was like any other ride. I wasn't
thinking of anything or expecting anything. Father
Hubert, Father Roman and I sat in the Buffalo station
talking about Rome, Paris, Cologne, and about *Life*
magazine being banned from St. Bonaventure library
for a couple of issues. About the big stuffed Buffalo,
about politics. The Baroness arrived and we started
back in the car.

Pretty soon the question comes up: "Are you going
into Catholic Action?"

Somehow I parry it.

About half an hour later: "When are you coming
to Friendship House?"

I parry by saying that I want to go on writing, and
that I would come on that condition.

She says: "Why?" And then adds that I should come
without any conditions or reservations.

Father Hubert says: "Why don't you just leave everything in her hands?"

I say, well, at least I have to stay at St. Bona's until mid-years, in February. Everyone laughs, and the matter is settled.

Sometimes I am in doubt about it, sometimes not. In any case I have until February to leave my mind a chance to change, in case there should be any reason for changing.

Before I had given Catherine my first argument (about wanting to write), I realized how foolish all the arguments would probably be.

That I am meant to stay here and teach!

That I am meant to stay here and pray and meditate a lot.

If I am supposed to write, then perhaps I will write more there than I would here, and to more purpose. If I am meant to teach—then the same will happen, I will teach better there. Pray and meditate—the same thing.

Yet I do not say I will do this or I will do that. I pray God that in February I may do His will and that between now and then I will invent no arguments to sell myself one idea or the other. I will continue praying and writing exactly as I am doing now.

No need for anything new, or for any excitement

whatever. If I pray, either I will change my mind or
I will not. In any case, God will guide me. No need
to be up in arms, no need to be anything other than
what I am—but I will pray and fast harder. No more
excitements, arguments, tearing of hair, trips to Cuba
and grandiose "farewell world" gestures. No need for
anything special—special joy or special sorrow, special
excitement or special torment. Everything is indiffer-
ent, except prayer, fasting, meditation—and work.
I thank God and all the saints that I am not running
around in circles—not yet. Defend me later, O God,
against all scruples!

¶ I got back from New York by the night train, having spent the night wedged into various positions in the hard green seats of the Erie daycoach. I am not physically tired, just filled with a deep, vague undefined sense of spiritual distress, as if I had a deep wound running inside me and it had to be stanched. As if I ought to go back to the chapel, or try to say something in a poem. The wound is only another aspect of the fact that we are exiles on this earth.

The sense of exile bleeds inside me like a hemorrhage. Always the same wound, whether a sense of sin or of holiness, or of one's own insufficiency, or of spiritual dryness. In the end, as we experience these things, they all end up by being pretty much the same wound. In fact, spiritual dryness is an acute experience of longing—therefore of love.

I got back to this wonderful, quiet place. There is a little snow on the hills, a light, hard-frozen powder.

The rooms are all silent. Water runs in the pipes.

It is still and peaceful, but there is no place for me here.

I am amazed at all this quietness which does not belong to me, and cannot. For a moment I get the illusion that the peace here is real, but it is not. It is merely the absence of trouble, not the peace of poverty and sacrifice. This "peace" cannot be enough for me any more.

Yet the place is beautiful and quiet. All the people who belong here are good. Their peace, no doubt, is genuine.

Yesterday, on retreat with the staff workers from Friendship House (Lax came also), Father Furfey said in one of the talks: "You will have to be despised by the world, and if you are not despised and rejected by it, there is something wrong! . . ." When he said that, I noticed the smile on the face of Betty S——. She smiled to herself like a kid that had been told something very pleasant, or invited out to a party. It was a nice, glad smile with more joy in it than I have seen anywhere else: a joy purified of merely earthly satisfaction!

¶ Aldous Huxley wrote a letter and sent five dollars for Friendship House. The more I think of this letter and his kindness, the more I am impressed by both. And the more I think of the article I wrote about him in the *Catholic World,* the more I regret it. In general, I may have been right in many things. But I made many glib and sweeping and self-complacent statements that I would gladly eat. One does not try to patronize a man like Huxley, even from the topmost point of St. Peter's dome. One smart statement that I regret was: "Huxley, as a philosopher, is not distinguished." Maybe so, but I would still gladly eat the words, because after all he has done a lot more thinking about important things than I ever have.

Four saints can make up for all the materialism in the world. Hitler, who thinks that the cupidity and materialism of some Catholics will enable him to destroy the Church, is crazy. He has not taken into account the sanctity that exists, though hidden, in the Church. Hitler is crazy to think that he can prevent people from manifesting the sanctity of the Church, by treating them as common criminals and preventing them from appearing to be martyrs. He thinks sanctity is a matter of appearances. He does not understand the supernatural meaning of sanctity. The saint has the strength of God in him. That is the only strength of the saint. It would be folly for Christians to rely on worldly means to combat dictators. There is only one defence: to take the Gospel literally, and to be *saints.*

¶ I spent most of the afternoon writing a letter to
Aldous Huxley and when I was finished I thought:
"Who am I to be telling this guy about mysticism?"
I reflect that until I read his book, *Ends and Means,*
four years ago, I had never even heard of the word
mysticism. The part he played in my conversion, by
that book, was very great. From Gilson's *Spirit of
Medieval Philosophy* I learned a healthy respect for
Catholicism. Then *Ends and Means* taught me to respect mysticism. Maritain's *Art and Scholasticism* was
another important influence, and Blake's poetry. Perhaps also Evelyn Underhill's *Mysticism,* though I read
precious little of it. I was fascinated by the Jesuit
sermons in Joyce's *A Portrait of the Artist as a Young
Man!* What horrified him, began to appeal to me. It
seemed to me quite sane. Finally G. F. Lahey's *Life
of Gerard Manley Hopkins;* I was reading about
Hopkins' conversion when I dropped the book and

268

ran out of the house to look for Father Ford. All this
reading covered a period of a year and a half or two
years—during which I read almost all of Father
Weiger's translations of Buddhist texts into French,
without understanding them.

Anyway, what do I know to *tell* Huxley? I should
have been asking him questions.

Today I think: should I be going to Harlem, or to
the Trappists? Why doesn't this idea of the Trappists
leave me? Should I do the thing I have wanted to do
since Spring, write and find out if the things the
Franciscans objected to might be passed over by the
Trappists?

If you were to ask me what I thought they would
answer, I would say I was almost certain they would
let me in. But perhaps what I am afraid of is to write
and be rejected, and have that last hope taken away—
as if it were a hope.

Would I not be obliged to admit, now, that if there
is a choice for me between Harlem and the Trappists,
I would not hesitate to take the Trappists? Is that why
I hesitate to find out if the choice exists? Is that my
roundabout way of evading my vocation?

I would have to renounce more in entering the
Trappists. That would be one place where I would

have to give up *everything*. Also anyone who believes
in the Mystical Body of Christ realizes I could do
more for the Church and for my brothers in the
world, if I were a Trappist at Gethsemani than if I
were a staff worker at Friendship House. Perhaps I
cling to my independence, to the chance to write, to
go where I like in the world . . . I must be prepared
to give all these things up. It seems monstrous at the
moment that I should consider my writing important
enough even to enter into the question. If God wants
me to write, I can write anywhere.

Harlem will be full of confusions. I don't particularly like the idea of working with a lot of girls.

Going to live in Harlem does not seem to me to be
anything special. It is a good and reasonable way to
follow Christ. But going to the Trappists is exciting,
it fills me with awe and with desire. I return to the
idea again and again: "Give up *everything*, give up
everything!"

I shall speak to one of the Friars.